50 Cheese Making Recipes for Home

By: Kelly Johnson

Table of Contents

- Ricotta Cheese
- Mozzarella Cheese
- Cheddar Cheese
- Brie Cheese
- Camembert Cheese
- Gouda Cheese
- Feta Cheese
- Parmesan Cheese
- Blue Cheese
- Halloumi Cheese
- Cottage Cheese
- Provolone Cheese
- Swiss Cheese
- Monterey Jack Cheese
- Havarti Cheese
- Colby Cheese
- Pepper Jack Cheese
- Emmental Cheese
- Manchego Cheese
- Fontina Cheese
- Limburger Cheese
- Muenster Cheese
- Taleggio Cheese
- Asiago Cheese
- Ricotta Salata Cheese
- Pecorino Romano Cheese
- Gruyère Cheese
- Roquefort Cheese
- Raclette Cheese
- Stilton Cheese
- Gorgonzola Cheese
- Edam Cheese
- Jarlsberg Cheese
- Provolone Cheese
- Burrata Cheese
- Quark Cheese
- Tilsit Cheese
- Fromage Blanc Cheese
- Reblochon Cheese
- Red Leicester Cheese

- Wensleydale Cheese
- Double Gloucester Cheese
- Saint André Cheese
- Pont-l'Évêque Cheese
- Cambozola Cheese
- Red Windsor Cheese
- Sage Derby Cheese
- Caerphilly Cheese
- Dunlop Cheese
- Coolea Cheese

Ricotta Cheese

Ingredients:

- 4 cups whole milk
- 2 cups heavy cream
- 1 teaspoon salt
- 3 tablespoons freshly squeezed lemon juice or white vinegar

Instructions:

1. In a large pot, combine the whole milk, heavy cream, and salt. Place the pot over medium heat and slowly bring the mixture to a gentle simmer, stirring occasionally to prevent scorching.
2. Once the mixture reaches a simmer, add the lemon juice or white vinegar. Stir gently to combine.
3. Reduce the heat to low and continue to simmer the mixture for 1-2 minutes, or until you see curds begin to form and separate from the whey.
4. Remove the pot from the heat and let it sit undisturbed for 5-10 minutes to allow the curds to further develop.
5. Line a large colander with cheesecloth and place it over a bowl or in the sink. Carefully pour the curds and whey mixture into the colander, allowing the whey to drain away.
6. Once most of the whey has drained off, gather the corners of the cheesecloth and tie them together to form a bundle. Hang the bundle over a bowl or sink faucet and let it drain for 15-30 minutes, or until the desired consistency is reached.
7. Untie the cheesecloth bundle and transfer the fresh ricotta cheese to a storage container. Use immediately or refrigerate for later use.

Enjoy your homemade ricotta cheese in pasta dishes, on toast, or as a filling for desserts like cannoli or cheesecake!

Mozzarella Cheese

Ingredients:

- 1 gallon whole milk (avoid ultra-pasteurized milk)
- 1 1/2 teaspoons citric acid
- 1/4 teaspoon liquid rennet diluted in 1/4 cup cool, chlorine-free water
- 1 teaspoon cheese salt or kosher salt

Instructions:

1. Prepare Ingredients: Dissolve the citric acid in 1/4 cup of cool water. Dilute the liquid rennet in another 1/4 cup of cool water.
2. Heat the Milk: Pour the gallon of milk into a large, non-reactive pot. Stir in the dissolved citric acid solution. Warm the milk over medium heat to 90°F (32°C), stirring occasionally to prevent scorching.
3. Add the Rennet: Once the milk reaches 90°F, remove it from the heat. Gently stir in the diluted rennet solution with an up-and-down motion for about 30 seconds.
4. Let the Curds Form: Cover the pot and let it sit undisturbed for 5-10 minutes, allowing the curds to form. You should see a clear separation between the curds and whey.
5. Cut the Curds: Using a long knife, cut the curds into a 1-inch checkerboard pattern. Be gentle to avoid breaking up the curds too much.
6. Heat the Curds: Return the pot to the stove and heat the curds over medium-low heat to 105°F (40°C), stirring gently to prevent sticking.
7. Remove Curds from Heat: Once the curds reach 105°F, remove the pot from the heat and continue stirring for another 5 minutes.
8. Drain the Curds: Use a slotted spoon to transfer the curds to a microwave-safe bowl, leaving the whey behind. Press the curds gently to remove excess whey.
9. Microwave and Stretch: Microwave the curds on high for 1 minute. Drain off any whey that accumulates. Put on gloves to handle the hot cheese. Stretch and fold the cheese, then return it to the microwave for another 30 seconds. Repeat until the cheese is smooth and shiny, typically 2-3 rounds of microwaving.
10. Form the Cheese: Once the cheese is smooth and stretchy, shape it into a ball or desired shape. Sprinkle with cheese salt or kosher salt and knead it into the cheese.
11. Enjoy or Store: Use the mozzarella immediately while it's warm and fresh, or store it in an airtight container in the refrigerator for up to a week.

Enjoy your homemade mozzarella on pizzas, salads, or simply drizzled with olive oil and balsamic vinegar!

Cheddar Cheese

Ingredients:

- 2 gallons whole milk (avoid ultra-pasteurized milk)
- 1/4 teaspoon mesophilic starter culture
- 1/2 teaspoon liquid rennet diluted in 1/4 cup cool, chlorine-free water
- 1 tablespoon cheese salt or kosher salt

Instructions:

1. Prepare Ingredients: Make sure all your equipment is clean and sanitized. Dissolve the mesophilic starter culture in 1/4 cup of cool, non-chlorinated water and set it aside. Dilute the liquid rennet in another 1/4 cup of cool, non-chlorinated water.
2. Heat the Milk: Pour the 2 gallons of milk into a large, non-reactive pot. Warm the milk over medium heat to 90°F (32°C), stirring occasionally to prevent scorching.
3. Add the Starter Culture: Once the milk reaches 90°F, remove it from the heat. Stir in the dissolved mesophilic starter culture with an up-and-down motion for about 30 seconds.
4. Add the Rennet: Gently stir in the diluted rennet solution for about 30 seconds to distribute it evenly throughout the milk.
5. Let the Curds Form: Cover the pot and let it sit undisturbed at room temperature for about 45-60 minutes, or until you achieve a clean break. The curds should have set and separated from the whey.
6. Cut the Curds: Use a long knife to cut the curds into small, uniform pieces, about the size of peas.
7. Cook the Curds: Place the pot back on the stove and heat the curds over medium-low heat, stirring gently to prevent sticking. Slowly raise the temperature to 100°F (38°C) over the course of 30 minutes, stirring frequently.
8. Stir and Rest the Curds: Once the curds reach 100°F, continue stirring for another 30 minutes. Then, let the curds rest undisturbed for 5 minutes.
9. Drain the Whey: Line a large colander with cheesecloth and place it over a clean sink or a large bowl. Carefully ladle the curds into the colander to drain off the whey.
10. Cheddarize the Curds: Transfer the drained curds back into the pot and stir in the cheese salt or kosher salt, making sure it's evenly distributed. Press the curds together with your hands to form a cohesive mass.
11. Press the Cheese: Line a cheese press or a DIY cheese press with cheesecloth and transfer the cheese curds into it. Press the cheese at 20 pounds of pressure for 20 minutes.
12. Flip and Press Again: After 20 minutes, remove the cheese from the press, unwrap it, and flip it over. Re-wrap the cheese in fresh cheesecloth and press it again at 40 pounds of pressure for 12 hours or overnight.
13. Air Dry and Age: Once pressed, remove the cheese from the press and let it air dry at room temperature for 1-2 days, or until the surface feels dry to the touch. Then, transfer the cheese

to a cheese cave or refrigerator to age for at least 1 month, preferably longer for a sharper flavor.
14. Enjoy: Your homemade cheddar cheese is now ready to be enjoyed! Slice it, shred it, or use it in your favorite recipes. Enjoy the delicious taste of your homemade cheese!

Brie Cheese

Ingredients:

- 2 gallons whole milk (avoid ultra-pasteurized milk)
- 1/4 teaspoon mesophilic starter culture
- 1/4 teaspoon liquid calcium chloride (if using pasteurized milk)
- 1/8 teaspoon liquid rennet diluted in 1/4 cup cool, chlorine-free water
- 1/4 cup cool, chlorine-free water
- Cheese salt or kosher salt

Instructions:

1. Prepare Ingredients: Make sure all your equipment is clean and sanitized. Dissolve the mesophilic starter culture in 1/4 cup of cool, non-chlorinated water and set it aside. If using pasteurized milk, dissolve the liquid calcium chloride in the same amount of water.
2. Heat the Milk: Pour the 2 gallons of milk into a large, non-reactive pot. Warm the milk over medium heat to 90°F (32°C), stirring occasionally to prevent scorching.
3. Add Starter Culture: Once the milk reaches 90°F, remove it from the heat. Stir in the dissolved mesophilic starter culture (and calcium chloride, if using) with an up-and-down motion for about 30 seconds.
4. Add the Rennet: Gently stir in the diluted rennet solution for about 30 seconds to distribute it evenly throughout the milk.
5. Let the Curds Form: Cover the pot and let it sit undisturbed at room temperature for about 45-60 minutes, or until you achieve a clean break. The curds should have set and separated from the whey.
6. Cut the Curds: Use a long knife to cut the curds into small, uniform pieces, about the size of peas.
7. Stir and Cook the Curds: Place the pot back on the stove and gently heat the curds over low heat, stirring gently to prevent sticking. Slowly raise the temperature to 100°F (38°C) over the course of 30 minutes, stirring frequently.
8. Drain the Whey: Line a large colander with cheesecloth and place it over a clean sink or a large bowl. Carefully ladle the curds into the colander to drain off the whey.
9. Salt the Curds: Transfer the drained curds into a large mixing bowl and sprinkle them with cheese salt or kosher salt. Gently toss the curds to distribute the salt evenly.
10. Mold the Cheese: Line a Brie cheese mold with cheesecloth and transfer the salted curds into it. Press the curds gently into the mold, smoothing the surface.
11. Press the Cheese: Fold the excess cheesecloth over the top of the cheese and place a follower or plate on top. Place a weight on the follower to press the cheese at a light pressure for 12-24 hours, depending on desired firmness.

12. Air Dry: After pressing, remove the cheese from the mold and carefully peel away the cheesecloth. Place the cheese on a cheese mat or rack in a cool, humid place to air dry for 12-24 hours, or until the surface feels dry to the touch.
13. Wrap and Age: Once dry, wrap the cheese in cheese paper or waxed paper and place it in the refrigerator to age. Brie cheese is typically aged for 2-4 weeks at temperatures around 50-55°F (10-13°C). During this time, the cheese will develop its characteristic bloomy rind.
14. Enjoy: Your homemade Brie cheese is now ready to be enjoyed! Serve it at room temperature with crusty bread, fruit, and nuts for a delightful cheese platter. Enjoy the creamy, luxurious taste of your homemade Brie!

Camembert Cheese

Ingredients:

- 2 gallons whole milk (avoid ultra-pasteurized milk)
- 1/4 teaspoon mesophilic starter culture
- 1/8 teaspoon Penicillium camemberti mold powder
- 1/4 teaspoon liquid calcium chloride (if using pasteurized milk)
- 1/8 teaspoon liquid rennet diluted in 1/4 cup cool, chlorine-free water
- 1/4 cup cool, chlorine-free water
- Cheese salt or kosher salt

Instructions:

1. Prepare Ingredients: Make sure all your equipment is clean and sanitized. Dissolve the mesophilic starter culture in 1/4 cup of cool, non-chlorinated water and set it aside. Dissolve the Penicillium camemberti mold powder in a small amount of cool, non-chlorinated water and set it aside. If using pasteurized milk, dissolve the liquid calcium chloride in the same amount of water.
2. Heat the Milk: Pour the 2 gallons of milk into a large, non-reactive pot. Warm the milk over medium heat to 86°F (30°C), stirring occasionally to prevent scorching.
3. Add Starter Culture and Mold: Once the milk reaches 86°F, remove it from the heat. Stir in the dissolved mesophilic starter culture and Penicillium camemberti mold solution (and calcium chloride, if using) with an up-and-down motion for about 30 seconds.
4. Add the Rennet: Gently stir in the diluted rennet solution for about 30 seconds to distribute it evenly throughout the milk.
5. Let the Curds Form: Cover the pot and let it sit undisturbed at room temperature for about 60-90 minutes, or until you achieve a clean break. The curds should have set and separated from the whey.
6. Cut the Curds: Use a long knife to cut the curds into small, uniform pieces, about the size of peas.
7. Stir and Cook the Curds: Place the pot back on the stove and gently heat the curds over low heat, stirring gently to prevent sticking. Slowly raise the temperature to 98°F (37°C) over the course of 30 minutes, stirring frequently.
8. Drain the Whey: Line a large colander with cheesecloth and place it over a clean sink or a large bowl. Carefully ladle the curds into the colander to drain off the whey.
9. Salt the Curds: Transfer the drained curds into a large mixing bowl and sprinkle them with cheese salt or kosher salt. Gently toss the curds to distribute the salt evenly.
10. Mold the Cheese: Line Camembert cheese molds with cheesecloth and transfer the salted curds into them. Press the curds gently into the molds, smoothing the surface.

11. Incubate the Cheese: Place the filled molds in a warm, humid environment, ideally at around 72°F (22°C) with high humidity (around 90%). Allow the cheese to incubate for 12-24 hours, or until a thin white mold begins to form on the surface.
12. Flip and Incubate Again: After the white mold has started to form, carefully remove the cheese from the molds and flip them. Return the cheeses to the incubation environment and continue to incubate until the mold covers the entire surface, typically another 12-24 hours.
13. Age the Cheese: Once fully coated in mold, transfer the cheeses to a cheese cave or refrigerator to age. Camembert cheese is typically aged for 3-4 weeks at temperatures around 50-55°F (10-13°C). During this time, the cheese will continue to develop its characteristic bloomy rind and creamy texture.
14. Enjoy: Your homemade Camembert cheese is now ready to be enjoyed! Serve it at room temperature with crusty bread, fruit, and nuts for a delightful cheese platter. Enjoy the creamy, luxurious taste of your homemade Camembert!

Gouda Cheese

Ingredients:

- 2 gallons whole milk (avoid ultra-pasteurized milk)
- 1/4 teaspoon mesophilic starter culture
- 1/8 teaspoon liquid calcium chloride (if using pasteurized milk)
- 1/4 teaspoon liquid rennet diluted in 1/4 cup cool, chlorine-free water
- 1/4 cup cool, chlorine-free water
- Cheese salt or kosher salt
- Cheese wax or vacuum-seal bags (for aging)

Instructions:

1. Prepare Ingredients: Make sure all your equipment is clean and sanitized. Dissolve the mesophilic starter culture in 1/4 cup of cool, non-chlorinated water and set it aside. If using pasteurized milk, dissolve the liquid calcium chloride in the same amount of water.
2. Heat the Milk: Pour the 2 gallons of milk into a large, non-reactive pot. Warm the milk over medium heat to 90°F (32°C), stirring occasionally to prevent scorching.
3. Add Starter Culture: Once the milk reaches 90°F, remove it from the heat. Stir in the dissolved mesophilic starter culture (and calcium chloride, if using) with an up-and-down motion for about 30 seconds.
4. Add the Rennet: Gently stir in the diluted rennet solution for about 30 seconds to distribute it evenly throughout the milk.
5. Let the Curds Form: Cover the pot and let it sit undisturbed at room temperature for about 45-60 minutes, or until you achieve a clean break. The curds should have set and separated from the whey.
6. Cut the Curds: Use a long knife to cut the curds into small, uniform pieces, about the size of peas.
7. Stir and Cook the Curds: Place the pot back on the stove and gently heat the curds over low heat, stirring gently to prevent sticking. Slowly raise the temperature to 102°F (39°C) over the course of 30 minutes, stirring frequently.
8. Cook the Curds: Once the curds reach 102°F, continue to cook them at this temperature for another 30 minutes, stirring gently to prevent matting.
9. Drain the Whey: Line a large colander with cheesecloth and place it over a clean sink or a large bowl. Carefully ladle the curds into the colander to drain off the whey.
10. Press the Curds: Transfer the drained curds into a cheese press lined with cheesecloth. Press the curds at 10 pounds of pressure for 15 minutes.
11. Flip and Press Again: After 15 minutes, remove the cheese from the press, flip it over, re-wrap it in fresh cheesecloth, and press it again at 20 pounds of pressure for 30 minutes.

12. Brine the Cheese: Prepare a brine solution by dissolving 2 tablespoons of cheese salt in 1 quart of cool, non-chlorinated water. Once pressed, place the cheese in the brine and let it soak for 12 hours, flipping it halfway through.
13. Air Dry: After brining, remove the cheese from the brine and pat it dry with paper towels. Place the cheese on a cheese mat or rack in a cool, humid place to air dry for 2-3 days, or until the surface feels dry to the touch.
14. Wax or Age: Once dry, coat the cheese with cheese wax or vacuum-seal it in bags for aging. Age the cheese at temperatures around 50-55°F (10-13°C) for 2-6 months, depending on desired flavor and texture.
15. Enjoy: Your homemade Gouda cheese is now ready to be enjoyed! Slice it, shred it, or use it in your favorite recipes. Enjoy the rich, nutty flavor of your homemade Gouda!

Feta Cheese

Ingredients:

- 2 gallons whole milk (avoid ultra-pasteurized milk)
- 1/4 teaspoon mesophilic starter culture
- 1/4 teaspoon liquid calcium chloride (if using pasteurized milk)
- 1/4 teaspoon liquid rennet diluted in 1/4 cup cool, chlorine-free water
- 1/4 cup cool, chlorine-free water
- 1/4 cup cheese salt or kosher salt
- 1/4 cup non-iodized cheese salt for brining

Instructions:

1. Prepare Ingredients: Make sure all your equipment is clean and sanitized. Dissolve the mesophilic starter culture in 1/4 cup of cool, non-chlorinated water and set it aside. If using pasteurized milk, dissolve the liquid calcium chloride in the same amount of water.
2. Heat the Milk: Pour the 2 gallons of milk into a large, non-reactive pot. Warm the milk over medium heat to 86°F (30°C), stirring occasionally to prevent scorching.
3. Add Starter Culture: Once the milk reaches 86°F, remove it from the heat. Stir in the dissolved mesophilic starter culture (and calcium chloride, if using) with an up-and-down motion for about 30 seconds.
4. Add the Rennet: Gently stir in the diluted rennet solution for about 30 seconds to distribute it evenly throughout the milk.
5. Let the Curds Form: Cover the pot and let it sit undisturbed at room temperature for about 60-90 minutes, or until you achieve a clean break. The curds should have set and separated from the whey.
6. Cut the Curds: Use a long knife to cut the curds into small, uniform pieces, about the size of peas.
7. Stir and Cook the Curds: Place the pot back on the stove and gently heat the curds over low heat, stirring gently to prevent sticking. Slowly raise the temperature to 100°F (38°C) over the course of 30 minutes, stirring frequently.
8. Drain the Whey: Line a large colander with cheesecloth and place it over a clean sink or a large bowl. Carefully ladle the curds into the colander to drain off the whey.
9. Salt the Curds: Transfer the drained curds into a large mixing bowl and sprinkle them with cheese salt or kosher salt. Gently toss the curds to distribute the salt evenly.
10. Mold the Cheese: Line a cheese mold with cheesecloth and transfer the salted curds into it. Press the curds gently into the mold, smoothing the surface.
11. Press the Cheese: Place a follower or plate on top of the cheese and press it at a light pressure for 6-8 hours, changing the cheesecloth and flipping the cheese halfway through.

12. Brine the Cheese: Prepare a brine solution by dissolving 1/4 cup of non-iodized cheese salt in 1 quart of cool, non-chlorinated water. Once pressed, place the cheese in the brine and let it soak for 8-12 hours, flipping it halfway through.
13. Age the Cheese: After brining, transfer the cheese to a cheese cave or refrigerator to age. Feta cheese is typically aged for 4-6 weeks at temperatures around 50-55°F (10-13°C). During this time, the cheese will develop its characteristic tangy flavor and crumbly texture.
14. Enjoy: Your homemade Feta cheese is now ready to be enjoyed! Crumble it over salads, pasta, or enjoy it on its own with olive oil and herbs. Enjoy the tangy, creamy taste of your homemade Feta!

Parmesan Cheese

Ingredients:

- 2 gallons whole milk (avoid ultra-pasteurized milk)
- 1/4 teaspoon thermophilic starter culture
- 1/4 teaspoon liquid calcium chloride (if using pasteurized milk)
- 1/4 teaspoon liquid rennet diluted in 1/4 cup cool, chlorine-free water
- 1/4 cup cool, chlorine-free water
- Cheese salt or kosher salt

Instructions:

1. Prepare Ingredients: Make sure all your equipment is clean and sanitized. Dissolve the thermophilic starter culture in 1/4 cup of cool, non-chlorinated water and set it aside. If using pasteurized milk, dissolve the liquid calcium chloride in the same amount of water.
2. Heat the Milk: Pour the 2 gallons of milk into a large, non-reactive pot. Warm the milk over medium heat to 104°F (40°C), stirring occasionally to prevent scorching.
3. Add Starter Culture: Once the milk reaches 104°F, remove it from the heat. Stir in the dissolved thermophilic starter culture (and calcium chloride, if using) with an up-and-down motion for about 30 seconds.
4. Add the Rennet: Gently stir in the diluted rennet solution for about 30 seconds to distribute it evenly throughout the milk.
5. Let the Curds Form: Cover the pot and let it sit undisturbed at room temperature for about 30-45 minutes, or until you achieve a clean break. The curds should have set and separated from the whey.
6. Cut the Curds: Use a long knife to cut the curds into small, uniform pieces, about the size of rice grains.
7. Stir and Cook the Curds: Place the pot back on the stove and gently heat the curds over low heat, stirring gently to prevent sticking. Slowly raise the temperature to 126°F (52°C) over the course of 30 minutes, stirring frequently.
8. Cook the Curds: Once the curds reach 126°F, continue to cook them at this temperature for another 30 minutes, stirring gently to prevent matting.
9. Drain the Whey: Line a large colander with cheesecloth and place it over a clean sink or a large bowl. Carefully ladle the curds into the colander to drain off the whey.

10. Press the Curds: Transfer the drained curds into a cheese mold lined with cheesecloth. Press the curds at 20 pounds of pressure for 15 minutes.
11. Flip and Press Again: After 15 minutes, remove the cheese from the mold, flip it over, re-wrap it in fresh cheesecloth, and press it again at 40 pounds of pressure for 12 hours.
12. Salt the Cheese: After pressing, remove the cheese from the mold and unwrap it. Rub the surface of the cheese with cheese salt or kosher salt.
13. Age the Cheese: Place the salted cheese on a cheese mat or rack in a cool, humid place to age. Parmesan cheese requires long-term aging, typically around 10-12 months or longer, at temperatures around 55-60°F (13-16°C) and high humidity (around 75-80%).
14. Enjoy: Your homemade Parmesan cheese is now ready to be enjoyed! Grate it over pasta, risotto, or salads, or enjoy it on its own with a glass of wine. Enjoy the rich, nutty flavor of your homemade Parmesan!

Blue Cheese

Ingredients:

- 2 gallons whole milk (avoid ultra-pasteurized milk)
- 1/4 teaspoon mesophilic starter culture
- 1/8 teaspoon Penicillium roqueforti mold powder
- 1/4 teaspoon liquid calcium chloride (if using pasteurized milk)
- 1/4 teaspoon liquid rennet diluted in 1/4 cup cool, chlorine-free water
- 1/4 cup cool, chlorine-free water
- Cheese salt or kosher salt

Instructions:

1. Prepare Ingredients: Ensure all equipment is clean and sanitized. Dissolve the mesophilic starter culture in 1/4 cup of cool, non-chlorinated water. Dissolve the Penicillium roqueforti mold powder in a small amount of cool, non-chlorinated water. If using pasteurized milk, dissolve the liquid calcium chloride in the same amount of water.
2. Heat the Milk: Pour the 2 gallons of milk into a large, non-reactive pot. Warm the milk over medium heat to 86°F (30°C), stirring occasionally to prevent scorching.
3. Add Starter Culture and Mold: Once the milk reaches 86°F, remove it from the heat. Stir in the dissolved mesophilic starter culture, Penicillium roqueforti mold solution (and calcium chloride, if using) with an up-and-down motion for about 30 seconds.
4. Add the Rennet: Gently stir in the diluted rennet solution for about 30 seconds to distribute it evenly throughout the milk.
5. Let the Curds Form: Cover the pot and let it sit undisturbed at room temperature for about 60-90 minutes, or until you achieve a clean break. The curds should have set and separated from the whey.
6. Cut the Curds: Use a long knife to cut the curds into small, uniform pieces, about the size of peas.
7. Stir and Cook the Curds: Place the pot back on the stove and gently heat the curds over low heat, stirring gently to prevent sticking. Slowly raise the temperature to 100°F (38°C) over the course of 30 minutes, stirring frequently.
8. Drain the Whey: Line a large colander with cheesecloth and place it over a clean sink or a large bowl. Carefully ladle the curds into the colander to drain off the whey.

9. Salt the Curds: Transfer the drained curds into a large mixing bowl and sprinkle them with cheese salt or kosher salt. Gently toss the curds to distribute the salt evenly.
10. Mold the Cheese: Line a cheese mold with cheesecloth and transfer the salted curds into it. Press the curds gently into the mold, smoothing the surface.
11. Incubate the Cheese: Place the filled mold in a warm, humid environment, ideally at around 70°F (21°C) with high humidity (around 90%). Allow the cheese to incubate for 24 hours.
12. Pierce the Cheese: After 24 hours, remove the cheese from the mold and pierce it all over with a sterilized skewer or knitting needle. This allows air to enter the cheese and encourages the growth of blue mold.
13. Age the Cheese: Return the pierced cheese to the warm, humid environment and continue to age it for another 4-6 weeks. During this time, the blue mold will grow and spread throughout the cheese, creating the characteristic veins of a blue cheese.
14. Enjoy: Your homemade Blue Cheese is now ready to be enjoyed! Serve it on a cheese platter, crumble it over salads, or use it in your favorite recipes for a bold, tangy flavor. Enjoy the creamy texture and complex taste of your homemade Blue Cheese!

Halloumi Cheese

Ingredients:

- 2 gallons whole milk (avoid ultra-pasteurized milk)
- 1/4 teaspoon mesophilic starter culture
- 1/4 teaspoon liquid calcium chloride (if using pasteurized milk)
- 1/4 teaspoon liquid rennet diluted in 1/4 cup cool, chlorine-free water
- 1/4 cup cool, chlorine-free water
- Cheese salt or kosher salt

Instructions:

1. Prepare Ingredients: Ensure all equipment is clean and sanitized. Dissolve the mesophilic starter culture in 1/4 cup of cool, non-chlorinated water. If using pasteurized milk, dissolve the liquid calcium chloride in the same amount of water.
2. Heat the Milk: Pour the 2 gallons of milk into a large, non-reactive pot. Warm the milk over medium heat to 86°F (30°C), stirring occasionally to prevent scorching.
3. Add Starter Culture: Once the milk reaches 86°F, remove it from the heat. Stir in the dissolved mesophilic starter culture (and calcium chloride, if using) with an up-and-down motion for about 30 seconds.
4. Add the Rennet: Gently stir in the diluted rennet solution for about 30 seconds to distribute it evenly throughout the milk.
5. Let the Curds Form: Cover the pot and let it sit undisturbed at room temperature for about 45-60 minutes, or until you achieve a clean break. The curds should have set and separated from the whey.
6. Cut the Curds: Use a long knife to cut the curds into small, uniform pieces, about the size of peas.
7. Cook the Curds: Place the pot back on the stove and gently heat the curds over low heat, stirring gently to prevent sticking. Slowly raise the temperature to 100°F (38°C) over the course of 30 minutes, stirring frequently.
8. Drain the Whey: Line a large colander with cheesecloth and place it over a clean sink or a large bowl. Carefully ladle the curds into the colander to drain off the whey.
9. Salt the Curds: Transfer the drained curds into a large mixing bowl and sprinkle them with cheese salt or kosher salt. Gently toss the curds to distribute the salt evenly.
10. Mold the Cheese: Line a cheese mold with cheesecloth and transfer the salted curds into it. Press the curds gently into the mold, smoothing the surface.
11. Press the Cheese: Place a follower or plate on top of the cheese and press it at a light pressure for 1-2 hours.
12. Slice and Cook the Cheese: After pressing, slice the cheese into pieces about 1/2 inch thick. Heat a skillet or grill pan over medium-high heat and cook the cheese slices for 2-3 minutes on each side, or until golden brown.

13. Serve: Your homemade Halloumi Cheese is now ready to be enjoyed! Serve it warm as an appetizer or side dish, drizzled with olive oil and garnished with fresh herbs. Enjoy the delicious taste and squeaky texture of your homemade Halloumi Cheese!

Cottage Cheese

Ingredients:

- 1 gallon whole milk (avoid ultra-pasteurized milk)
- 1/4 cup white vinegar or lemon juice
- 1 teaspoon salt (optional)

Instructions:

1. Heat the Milk: Pour the gallon of milk into a large, heavy-bottomed pot. Heat the milk over medium heat, stirring frequently to prevent scorching, until it reaches around 195°F (90°C). You'll start to see steam rising from the surface of the milk.
2. Add the Acid: Once the milk reaches the desired temperature, remove it from the heat. Slowly pour in the white vinegar or lemon juice while gently stirring the milk. Continue stirring for a minute to ensure the acid is evenly distributed.
3. Let the Curds Form: Cover the pot and let it sit undisturbed for about 10-15 minutes. During this time, the milk will curdle, and you'll see the curds separating from the whey. If the curds are too small, let it sit for a few more minutes.
4. Drain the Curds: Line a large colander with cheesecloth or a clean kitchen towel and place it over a large bowl or in the sink. Carefully pour the curdled milk into the colander to separate the curds from the whey. Let it drain for a few minutes.
5. Rinse the Curds (Optional): If you prefer a milder flavor, you can rinse the curds under cold water to remove some of the acidity from the vinegar or lemon juice.
6. Season the Curds (Optional): If desired, sprinkle the curds with salt and gently mix it in to enhance the flavor.
7. Serve or Store: Your homemade cottage cheese is now ready to be enjoyed! You can serve it immediately while it's still warm or refrigerate it in an airtight container for up to one week.
8. Enjoy: Serve your cottage cheese plain, with fresh fruit, or mixed with herbs and spices for added flavor. It's versatile and can be enjoyed in various dishes or simply on its own as a nutritious snack.

Provolone Cheese

Ingredients:

- 2 gallons whole milk (avoid ultra-pasteurized milk)
- 1/4 teaspoon mesophilic starter culture
- 1/4 teaspoon liquid calcium chloride (if using pasteurized milk)
- 1/4 teaspoon liquid rennet diluted in 1/4 cup cool, chlorine-free water
- 1/4 cup cool, chlorine-free water
- Cheese salt or kosher salt

Instructions:

1. Prepare Ingredients: Ensure all equipment is clean and sanitized. Dissolve the mesophilic starter culture in 1/4 cup of cool, non-chlorinated water. If using pasteurized milk, dissolve the liquid calcium chloride in the same amount of water.
2. Heat the Milk: Pour the 2 gallons of milk into a large, non-reactive pot. Warm the milk over medium heat to 90°F (32°C), stirring occasionally to prevent scorching.
3. Add Starter Culture: Once the milk reaches 90°F, remove it from the heat. Stir in the dissolved mesophilic starter culture (and calcium chloride, if using) with an up-and-down motion for about 30 seconds.
4. Add the Rennet: Gently stir in the diluted rennet solution for about 30 seconds to distribute it evenly throughout the milk.
5. Let the Curds Form: Cover the pot and let it sit undisturbed at room temperature for about 45-60 minutes, or until you achieve a clean break. The curds should have set and separated from the whey.
6. Cut the Curds: Use a long knife to cut the curds into small, uniform pieces, about the size of peas.
7. Stir and Cook the Curds: Place the pot back on the stove and gently heat the curds over low heat, stirring gently to prevent sticking. Slowly raise the temperature to 115°F (46°C) over the course of 30 minutes, stirring frequently.
8. Cook the Curds: Once the curds reach 115°F, continue to cook them at this temperature for another 30 minutes, stirring gently to prevent matting.
9. Drain the Whey: Line a large colander with cheesecloth and place it over a clean sink or a large bowl. Carefully ladle the curds into the colander to drain off the whey.

10. Salt the Curds: Transfer the drained curds into a large mixing bowl and sprinkle them with cheese salt or kosher salt. Gently toss the curds to distribute the salt evenly.
11. Mold the Cheese: Line a cheese mold with cheesecloth and transfer the salted curds into it. Press the curds gently into the mold, smoothing the surface.
12. Press the Cheese: Place a follower or plate on top of the cheese and press it at a light pressure for 2-3 hours.
13. Brine the Cheese (Optional): Prepare a brine solution by dissolving cheese salt in cool, non-chlorinated water. Once pressed, place the cheese in the brine and let it soak for 12-24 hours in the refrigerator.
14. Air Dry and Age: After brining (if desired), remove the cheese from the brine and pat it dry with paper towels. Place the cheese on a cheese mat or rack in a cool, humid place to air dry for 2-3 days, or until the surface feels dry to the touch. Then, transfer the cheese to a cheese cave or refrigerator to age for at least 2-3 months, preferably longer for a sharper flavor.
15. Enjoy: Your homemade Provolone cheese is now ready to be enjoyed! Slice it, shred it, or use it in your favorite recipes. Enjoy the rich, creamy taste of your homemade Provolone!

Swiss Cheese

Ingredients:

- 2 gallons whole milk (avoid ultra-pasteurized milk)
- 1/4 teaspoon mesophilic starter culture
- 1/4 teaspoon liquid calcium chloride (if using pasteurized milk)
- 1/4 teaspoon liquid rennet diluted in 1/4 cup cool, chlorine-free water
- 1/4 cup cool, chlorine-free water
- Cheese salt or kosher salt
- Propionic Shermanii culture (for the eyes characteristic of Swiss cheese)

Instructions:

1. Prepare Ingredients: Ensure all equipment is clean and sanitized. Dissolve the mesophilic starter culture in 1/4 cup of cool, non-chlorinated water. If using pasteurized milk, dissolve the liquid calcium chloride in the same amount of water. Prepare the liquid rennet and set it aside.
2. Heat the Milk: Pour the 2 gallons of milk into a large, non-reactive pot. Warm the milk over medium heat to 90°F (32°C), stirring occasionally to prevent scorching.
3. Add Starter Culture: Once the milk reaches 90°F, remove it from the heat. Stir in the dissolved mesophilic starter culture (and calcium chloride, if using) with an up-and-down motion for about 30 seconds.
4. Add the Rennet: Gently stir in the diluted rennet solution for about 30 seconds to distribute it evenly throughout the milk.
5. Let the Curds Form: Cover the pot and let it sit undisturbed at room temperature for about 30-45 minutes, or until you achieve a clean break. The curds should have set and separated from the whey.
6. Cut the Curds: Use a long knife to cut the curds into small, uniform pieces, about the size of peas.
7. Cook the Curds: Place the pot back on the stove and gently heat the curds over low heat, stirring gently to prevent sticking. Slowly raise the temperature to 130°F (54°C) over the course of 30 minutes, stirring frequently.
8. Drain the Whey: Line a large colander with cheesecloth and place it over a clean sink or a large bowl. Carefully ladle the curds into the colander to drain off the whey.
9. Press the Curds: Transfer the drained curds into a cheese mold lined with cheesecloth. Press the curds at 20 pounds of pressure for 30 minutes.
10. Cut and Stack the Curds: After the initial pressing, remove the cheese from the mold and cut it into smaller pieces. Restack the pieces on top of each other, flipping them every 15 minutes for 2 hours.
11. Add Propionic Shermanii Culture: Sprinkle the propionic Shermanii culture over the surface of the stacked curds and mix it in thoroughly.

12. Press Again: Return the stacked curds to the cheese mold, re-wrap them in cheesecloth, and press them at 40 pounds of pressure for 12 hours.
13. Brine the Cheese: After pressing, prepare a brine solution by dissolving cheese salt in cool, non-chlorinated water. Brine the cheese for 12 hours.
14. Air Dry and Age: After brining, pat the cheese dry with paper towels and let it air dry on a cheese mat or rack for 1-2 days at room temperature. Then, transfer it to a cheese cave or refrigerator to age for at least 2-3 months, preferably longer, at temperatures around 50-55°F (10-13°C) with high humidity.
15. Enjoy: Your homemade Swiss cheese is now ready to be enjoyed! Slice it thinly for sandwiches, shred it for fondue, or enjoy it on its own with crackers and fruit. Enjoy the nutty flavor and characteristic holes of your homemade Swiss cheese!

Monterey Jack Cheese

Ingredients:

- 2 gallons whole milk (avoid ultra-pasteurized milk)
- 1/4 teaspoon mesophilic starter culture
- 1/4 teaspoon liquid calcium chloride (if using pasteurized milk)
- 1/4 teaspoon liquid rennet diluted in 1/4 cup cool, chlorine-free water
- 1/4 cup cool, chlorine-free water
- Cheese salt or kosher salt

Instructions:

1. Prepare Ingredients: Ensure all equipment is clean and sanitized. Dissolve the mesophilic starter culture in 1/4 cup of cool, non-chlorinated water. If using pasteurized milk, dissolve the liquid calcium chloride in the same amount of water.
2. Heat the Milk: Pour the 2 gallons of milk into a large, non-reactive pot. Warm the milk over medium heat to 90°F (32°C), stirring occasionally to prevent scorching.
3. Add Starter Culture: Once the milk reaches 90°F, remove it from the heat. Stir in the dissolved mesophilic starter culture (and calcium chloride, if using) with an up-and-down motion for about 30 seconds.
4. Add the Rennet: Gently stir in the diluted rennet solution for about 30 seconds to distribute it evenly throughout the milk.
5. Let the Curds Form: Cover the pot and let it sit undisturbed at room temperature for about 45-60 minutes, or until you achieve a clean break. The curds should have set and separated from the whey.

6. Cut the Curds: Use a long knife to cut the curds into small, uniform pieces, about the size of peas.
7. Stir and Cook the Curds: Place the pot back on the stove and gently heat the curds over low heat, stirring gently to prevent sticking. Slowly raise the temperature to 100°F (38°C) over the course of 30 minutes, stirring frequently.
8. Drain the Whey: Line a large colander with cheesecloth and place it over a clean sink or a large bowl. Carefully ladle the curds into the colander to drain off the whey.
9. Salt the Curds: Transfer the drained curds into a large mixing bowl and sprinkle them with cheese salt or kosher salt. Gently toss the curds to distribute the salt evenly.
10. Mold the Cheese: Line a cheese mold with cheesecloth and transfer the salted curds into it. Press the curds gently into the mold, smoothing the surface.
11. Press the Cheese: Place a follower or plate on top of the cheese and press it at a light pressure for 2-3 hours.
12. Brine the Cheese (Optional): Prepare a brine solution by dissolving cheese salt in cool, non-chlorinated water. Once pressed, place the cheese in the brine and let it soak for 12-24 hours in the refrigerator.
13. Air Dry and Age (Optional): After brining (if desired), remove the cheese from the brine and pat it dry with paper towels. Allow the cheese to air dry on a cheese mat or rack in the refrigerator for 1-2 days, then enjoy it fresh or age it further for a firmer texture and stronger flavor.
14. Enjoy: Your homemade Monterey Jack cheese is now ready to be enjoyed! Slice it, shred it, or melt it in your favorite recipes. Enjoy the creamy texture and mild flavor of your homemade cheese!

Havarti Cheese

Ingredients:

- 2 gallons whole milk (avoid ultra-pasteurized milk)
- 1/4 teaspoon mesophilic starter culture
- 1/8 teaspoon liquid calcium chloride (if using pasteurized milk)
- 1/4 teaspoon liquid rennet diluted in 1/4 cup cool, chlorine-free water
- 1/4 cup cool, chlorine-free water
- Cheese salt or kosher salt
- Optional: Herbs or spices for flavor variation

Instructions:

1. Prepare Ingredients: Make sure all your equipment is clean and sanitized. Dissolve the mesophilic starter culture in 1/4 cup of cool, non-chlorinated water and set it aside. If using pasteurized milk, dissolve the liquid calcium chloride in the same amount of water.
2. Heat the Milk: Pour the 2 gallons of milk into a large, non-reactive pot. Warm the milk over medium heat to 86°F (30°C), stirring occasionally to prevent scorching.
3. Add Starter Culture: Once the milk reaches 86°F, remove it from the heat. Stir in the dissolved mesophilic starter culture (and calcium chloride, if using) with an up-and-down motion for about 30 seconds.
4. Add the Rennet: Gently stir in the diluted rennet solution for about 30 seconds to distribute it evenly throughout the milk.
5. Let the Curds Form: Cover the pot and let it sit undisturbed at room temperature for about 45-60 minutes, or until you achieve a clean break. The curds should have set and separated from the whey.
6. Cut the Curds: Use a long knife to cut the curds into small, uniform pieces, about the size of peas.
7. Stir and Cook the Curds: Place the pot back on the stove and gently heat the curds over low heat, stirring gently to prevent sticking. Slowly raise the temperature to 100°F (38°C) over the course of 30 minutes, stirring frequently.
8. Drain the Whey: Line a large colander with cheesecloth and place it over a clean sink or a large bowl. Carefully ladle the curds into the colander to drain off the whey.
9. Press the Curds: Transfer the drained curds into a cheese mold lined with cheesecloth. Press the curds at 20 pounds of pressure for 2 hours.
10. Salt the Cheese: After pressing, remove the cheese from the mold and sprinkle it with cheese salt or kosher salt. Optionally, you can add herbs or spices to flavor the cheese.
11. Age the Cheese (Optional): Transfer the salted cheese to a cheese cave or refrigerator to age for 4-6 weeks. During this time, the flavor of the cheese will develop and mature.

12. Enjoy: Your homemade Havarti cheese is now ready to be enjoyed! Slice it, shred it, or melt it in your favorite recipes. Enjoy the creamy texture and mild, buttery flavor of your homemade cheese!

Colby Cheese

Ingredients:

- 2 gallons whole milk (avoid ultra-pasteurized milk)
- 1/4 teaspoon mesophilic starter culture
- 1/8 teaspoon liquid calcium chloride (if using pasteurized milk)
- 1/4 teaspoon liquid rennet diluted in 1/4 cup cool, chlorine-free water
- 1/4 cup cool, chlorine-free water
- Cheese salt or kosher salt

Instructions:

1. Prepare Ingredients: Ensure all equipment is clean and sanitized. Dissolve the mesophilic starter culture in 1/4 cup of cool, non-chlorinated water and set it aside. If using pasteurized milk, dissolve the liquid calcium chloride in the same amount of water.
2. Heat the Milk: Pour the 2 gallons of milk into a large, non-reactive pot. Warm the milk over medium heat to 86°F (30°C), stirring occasionally to prevent scorching.
3. Add Starter Culture: Once the milk reaches 86°F, remove it from the heat. Stir in the dissolved mesophilic starter culture (and calcium chloride, if using) with an up-and-down motion for about 30 seconds.
4. Add the Rennet: Gently stir in the diluted rennet solution for about 30 seconds to distribute it evenly throughout the milk.
5. Let the Curds Form: Cover the pot and let it sit undisturbed at room temperature for about 45-60 minutes, or until you achieve a clean break. The curds should have set and separated from the whey.
6. Cut the Curds: Use a long knife to cut the curds into small, uniform pieces, about the size of peas.
7. Stir and Cook the Curds: Place the pot back on the stove and gently heat the curds over low heat, stirring gently to prevent sticking. Slowly raise the temperature to 100°F (38°C) over the course of 30 minutes, stirring frequently.
8. Drain the Whey: Line a large colander with cheesecloth and place it over a clean sink or a large bowl. Carefully ladle the curds into the colander to drain off the whey.

9. Cheddaring Process: Transfer the drained curds to a clean surface and allow them to cool slightly. Then, stack the curds on top of each other and flip them every 15 minutes for 1 hour.
10. Mill and Salt the Curds: After cheddaring, mill the curds into smaller pieces and sprinkle them with cheese salt or kosher salt. Mix the salt evenly through the curds.
11. Press the Cheese: Transfer the salted curds into a cheese mold lined with cheesecloth. Press the curds at 20 pounds of pressure for 2 hours.
12. Air Dry and Age: After pressing, remove the cheese from the mold and air dry it on a cheese mat or rack at room temperature for 1-2 days, or until the surface feels dry to the touch. Then, transfer the cheese to a cheese cave or refrigerator to age for at least 2-3 months, preferably longer, at temperatures around 50-55°F (10-13°C) with high humidity.
13. Enjoy: Your homemade Colby cheese is now ready to be enjoyed! Slice it, shred it, or melt it in your favorite recipes. Enjoy the creamy texture and mild, tangy flavor of your homemade cheese!

Pepper Jack Cheese

Ingredients:

- 2 gallons whole milk (avoid ultra-pasteurized milk)
- 1/4 teaspoon mesophilic starter culture
- 1/8 teaspoon liquid calcium chloride (if using pasteurized milk)
- 1/4 teaspoon liquid rennet diluted in 1/4 cup cool, chlorine-free water
- 1/4 cup cool, chlorine-free water
- 1-2 jalapeño peppers, finely chopped (seeds removed for milder flavor)
- Cheese salt or kosher salt

Instructions:

1. Prepare Ingredients: Ensure all equipment is clean and sanitized. Dissolve the mesophilic starter culture in 1/4 cup of cool, non-chlorinated water and set it aside. If using pasteurized milk, dissolve the liquid calcium chloride in the same amount of water. Finely chop the jalapeño peppers and set them aside.
2. Heat the Milk: Pour the 2 gallons of milk into a large, non-reactive pot. Warm the milk over medium heat to 86°F (30°C), stirring occasionally to prevent scorching.
3. Add Starter Culture: Once the milk reaches 86°F, remove it from the heat. Stir in the dissolved mesophilic starter culture (and calcium chloride, if using) with an up-and-down motion for about 30 seconds.
4. Add the Rennet: Gently stir in the diluted rennet solution for about 30 seconds to distribute it evenly throughout the milk.
5. Let the Curds Form: Cover the pot and let it sit undisturbed at room temperature for about 45-60 minutes, or until you achieve a clean break. The curds should have set and separated from the whey.
6. Cut the Curds: Use a long knife to cut the curds into small, uniform pieces, about the size of peas.
7. Stir and Cook the Curds: Place the pot back on the stove and gently heat the curds over low heat, stirring gently to prevent sticking. Slowly raise the temperature to 100°F (38°C) over the course of 30 minutes, stirring frequently.
8. Add Jalapeño Peppers: Once the curds reach 100°F, stir in the chopped jalapeño peppers until evenly distributed throughout the curds.
9. Drain the Whey: Line a large colander with cheesecloth and place it over a clean sink or a large bowl. Carefully ladle the curds into the colander to drain off the whey.
10. Salt the Curds: Transfer the drained curds into a large mixing bowl and sprinkle them with cheese salt or kosher salt. Gently toss the curds to distribute the salt evenly.
11. Mold the Cheese: Line a cheese mold with cheesecloth and transfer the salted curds into it. Press the curds gently into the mold, smoothing the surface.

12. Press the Cheese: Place a follower or plate on top of the cheese and press it at a light pressure for 2-3 hours.
13. Air Dry and Age (Optional): After pressing, remove the cheese from the mold and air dry it on a cheese mat or rack at room temperature for 1-2 days, or until the surface feels dry to the touch. Then, transfer the cheese to a cheese cave or refrigerator to age for at least 2-3 weeks for flavors to develop and meld.
14. Enjoy: Your homemade Pepper Jack cheese is now ready to be enjoyed! Slice it, shred it, or melt it in your favorite recipes. Enjoy the creamy texture and spicy kick of your homemade cheese! Adjust the amount of jalapeño peppers according to your preference for heat.

Emmental Cheese

Ingredients:

- 2 gallons whole milk (avoid ultra-pasteurized milk)
- 1/4 teaspoon mesophilic starter culture
- 1/8 teaspoon liquid calcium chloride (if using pasteurized milk)
- 1/4 teaspoon liquid rennet diluted in 1/4 cup cool, chlorine-free water
- 1/4 cup cool, chlorine-free water
- Cheese salt or kosher salt
- Propionic Shermanii culture (for the holes characteristic of Emmental cheese)

Instructions:

1. Prepare Ingredients: Ensure all equipment is clean and sanitized. Dissolve the mesophilic starter culture in 1/4 cup of cool, non-chlorinated water. If using pasteurized milk, dissolve the liquid calcium chloride in the same amount of water. Prepare the liquid rennet and set it aside.
2. Heat the Milk: Pour the 2 gallons of milk into a large, non-reactive pot. Warm the milk over medium heat to 86°F (30°C), stirring occasionally to prevent scorching.
3. Add Starter Culture: Once the milk reaches 86°F, remove it from the heat. Stir in the dissolved mesophilic starter culture (and calcium chloride, if using) with an up-and-down motion for about 30 seconds.
4. Add the Rennet: Gently stir in the diluted rennet solution for about 30 seconds to distribute it evenly throughout the milk.
5. Let the Curds Form: Cover the pot and let it sit undisturbed at room temperature for about 30-45 minutes, or until you achieve a clean break. The curds should have set and separated from the whey.
6. Cut the Curds: Use a long knife to cut the curds into small, uniform pieces, about the size of peas.
7. Stir and Cook the Curds: Place the pot back on the stove and gently heat the curds over low heat, stirring gently to prevent sticking. Slowly raise the temperature to 126°F (52°C) over the course of 30 minutes, stirring frequently.
8. Drain the Whey: Line a large colander with cheesecloth and place it over a clean sink or a large bowl. Carefully ladle the curds into the colander to drain off the whey.

9. Add Propionic Shermanii Culture: Sprinkle the propionic Shermanii culture over the surface of the drained curds and mix it in thoroughly. This culture is responsible for the formation of the characteristic holes in Emmental cheese.
10. Press the Curds: Transfer the curds to cheese molds lined with cheesecloth. Press the curds at gradually increasing pressure over several hours, starting from light pressure and gradually increasing to around 50 pounds over the course of 12 hours.
11. Brine the Cheese: After pressing, soak the cheese in a brine solution for 24-48 hours. The brine solution should be around 20-22% salt concentration.
12. Age the Cheese: Transfer the brined cheese to a cheese cave or refrigerator with a temperature of around 45-55°F (7-13°C) and high humidity. Age the cheese for at least 2-3 months, or longer for a stronger flavor and larger holes.
13. Enjoy: Your homemade Emmental cheese is now ready to be enjoyed! Slice it thinly for sandwiches, grate it for fondue, or enjoy it on its own with crackers and fruit. Revel in the nutty flavor and characteristic holes of your homemade Emmental cheese!

Manchego Cheese

Ingredients:

- 2 gallons whole milk (avoid ultra-pasteurized milk)
- 1/4 teaspoon mesophilic starter culture
- 1/4 teaspoon liquid calcium chloride (if using pasteurized milk)
- 1/4 teaspoon liquid rennet diluted in 1/4 cup cool, chlorine-free water
- 1/4 cup cool, chlorine-free water
- Cheese salt or kosher salt

Instructions:

1. Prepare Ingredients: Ensure all equipment is clean and sanitized. Dissolve the mesophilic starter culture in 1/4 cup of cool, non-chlorinated water. If using pasteurized milk, dissolve the liquid calcium chloride in the same amount of water. Prepare the liquid rennet and set it aside.
2. Heat the Milk: Pour the 2 gallons of milk into a large, non-reactive pot. Warm the milk over medium heat to 86°F (30°C), stirring occasionally to prevent scorching.
3. Add Starter Culture: Once the milk reaches 86°F, remove it from the heat. Stir in the dissolved mesophilic starter culture (and calcium chloride, if using) with an up-and-down motion for about 30 seconds.
4. Add the Rennet: Gently stir in the diluted rennet solution for about 30 seconds to distribute it evenly throughout the milk.
5. Let the Curds Form: Cover the pot and let it sit undisturbed at room temperature for about 45-60 minutes, or until you achieve a clean break. The curds should have set and separated from the whey.
6. Cut the Curds: Use a long knife to cut the curds into small, uniform pieces, about the size of peas.
7. Cook the Curds: Place the pot back on the stove and gently heat the curds over low heat, stirring gently to prevent sticking. Slowly raise the temperature to 104°F (40°C) over the course of 30 minutes, stirring frequently.
8. Drain the Whey: Line a large colander with cheesecloth and place it over a clean sink or a large bowl. Carefully ladle the curds into the colander to drain off the whey.
9. Salt the Curds: Transfer the drained curds into a large mixing bowl and sprinkle them with cheese salt or kosher salt. Gently toss the curds to distribute the salt evenly.
10. Mold the Cheese: Line a cheese mold with cheesecloth and transfer the salted curds into it. Press the curds gently into the mold, smoothing the surface.
11. Press the Cheese: Place a follower or plate on top of the cheese and press it at a light pressure for 12 hours.
12. Air Dry and Age: After pressing, remove the cheese from the mold and air dry it on a cheese mat or rack at room temperature for 1-2 days, or until the surface feels dry to the touch.

Then, transfer the cheese to a cheese cave or refrigerator to age for at least 2-3 months, preferably longer, at temperatures around 50-55°F (10-13°C) with high humidity.
13. Enjoy: Your homemade Manchego cheese is now ready to be enjoyed! Slice it thinly for sandwiches, grate it for salads, or enjoy it on its own with bread and fruit. Revel in the nutty flavor and firm texture of your homemade Manchego cheese!

Fontina Cheese

Ingredients:

- 2 gallons whole milk (avoid ultra-pasteurized milk)
- 1/4 teaspoon mesophilic starter culture
- 1/4 teaspoon liquid calcium chloride (if using pasteurized milk)
- 1/4 teaspoon liquid rennet diluted in 1/4 cup cool, chlorine-free water
- 1/4 cup cool, chlorine-free water
- Cheese salt or kosher salt

Instructions:

1. Prepare Ingredients: Ensure all equipment is clean and sanitized. Dissolve the mesophilic starter culture in 1/4 cup of cool, non-chlorinated water. If using pasteurized milk, dissolve the liquid calcium chloride in the same amount of water. Prepare the liquid rennet and set it aside.
2. Heat the Milk: Pour the 2 gallons of milk into a large, non-reactive pot. Warm the milk over medium heat to 90°F (32°C), stirring occasionally to prevent scorching.
3. Add Starter Culture: Once the milk reaches 90°F, remove it from the heat. Stir in the dissolved mesophilic starter culture (and calcium chloride, if using) with an up-and-down motion for about 30 seconds.
4. Add the Rennet: Gently stir in the diluted rennet solution for about 30 seconds to distribute it evenly throughout the milk.
5. Let the Curds Form: Cover the pot and let it sit undisturbed at room temperature for about 45-60 minutes, or until you achieve a clean break. The curds should have set and separated from the whey.
6. Cut the Curds: Use a long knife to cut the curds into small, uniform pieces, about the size of peas.
7. Stir and Cook the Curds: Place the pot back on the stove and gently heat the curds over low heat, stirring gently to prevent sticking. Slowly raise the temperature to 102°F (39°C) over the course of 30 minutes, stirring frequently.
8. Drain the Whey: Line a large colander with cheesecloth and place it over a clean sink or a large bowl. Carefully ladle the curds into the colander to drain off the whey.
9. Salt the Curds: Transfer the drained curds into a large mixing bowl and sprinkle them with cheese salt or kosher salt. Gently toss the curds to distribute the salt evenly.
10. Mold the Cheese: Line a cheese mold with cheesecloth and transfer the salted curds into it. Press the curds gently into the mold, smoothing the surface.
11. Press the Cheese: Place a follower or plate on top of the cheese and press it at a light pressure for 12 hours.
12. Air Dry and Age: After pressing, remove the cheese from the mold and air dry it on a cheese mat or rack at room temperature for 1-2 days, or until the surface feels dry to the touch.

Then, transfer the cheese to a cheese cave or refrigerator to age for at least 2-3 months, preferably longer, at temperatures around 45-50°F (7-10°C) with moderate humidity.

13. Enjoy: Your homemade Fontina cheese is now ready to be enjoyed! Slice it for sandwiches, melt it over pasta, or savor it on a cheese board with fruits and nuts. Enjoy the creamy texture and mild, nutty flavor of your homemade Fontina cheese!

Limburger Cheese

Ingredients:

- 2 gallons whole milk (avoid ultra-pasteurized milk)
- 1/4 teaspoon mesophilic starter culture
- 1/4 teaspoon Brevibacterium linens culture (specific to Limburger cheese)
- 1/4 teaspoon liquid calcium chloride (if using pasteurized milk)
- 1/4 teaspoon liquid rennet diluted in 1/4 cup cool, chlorine-free water
- 1/4 cup cool, chlorine-free water
- Cheese salt or kosher salt

Instructions:

1. Prepare Ingredients: Ensure all equipment is clean and sanitized. Dissolve the mesophilic starter culture and Brevibacterium linens culture in 1/4 cup of cool, non-chlorinated water each. If using pasteurized milk, dissolve the liquid calcium chloride in the same amount of water. Prepare the liquid rennet and set it aside.
2. Heat the Milk: Pour the 2 gallons of milk into a large, non-reactive pot. Warm the milk over medium heat to 90°F (32°C), stirring occasionally to prevent scorching.
3. Add Starter Cultures: Once the milk reaches 90°F, remove it from the heat. Stir in the dissolved mesophilic starter culture and Brevibacterium linens culture with an up-and-down motion for about 30 seconds.
4. Add the Rennet: Gently stir in the diluted rennet solution for about 30 seconds to distribute it evenly throughout the milk.
5. Let the Curds Form: Cover the pot and let it sit undisturbed at room temperature for about 45-60 minutes, or until you achieve a clean break. The curds should have set and separated from the whey.
6. Cut the Curds: Use a long knife to cut the curds into small, uniform pieces, about the size of peas.
7. Stir and Cook the Curds: Place the pot back on the stove and gently heat the curds over low heat, stirring gently to prevent sticking. Slowly raise the temperature to 102°F (39°C) over the course of 30 minutes, stirring frequently.
8. Drain the Whey: Line a large colander with cheesecloth and place it over a clean sink or a large bowl. Carefully ladle the curds into the colander to drain off the whey.
9. Salt the Curds: Transfer the drained curds into a large mixing bowl and sprinkle them with cheese salt or kosher salt. Gently toss the curds to distribute the salt evenly.
10. Mold the Cheese: Line cheese molds with cheesecloth and transfer the salted curds into them. Press the curds gently into the molds, smoothing the surface.
11. Press the Cheese: Place a follower or plate on top of the cheese in each mold and press them at a light pressure for 12 hours.

12. Age the Cheese: After pressing, transfer the cheeses to a cheese cave or refrigerator with a temperature of around 50-55°F (10-13°C) and high humidity. Age the cheese for at least 3-4 weeks, preferably longer, to develop its characteristic flavor and aroma.
13. Enjoy: Your homemade Limburger cheese is now ready to be enjoyed! Serve it on sandwiches, crackers, or with fruit. Embrace the pungent aroma and complex flavor of your homemade Limburger cheese!

Muenster Cheese

Ingredients:

- 2 gallons whole milk (avoid ultra-pasteurized milk)
- 1/4 teaspoon mesophilic starter culture
- 1/4 teaspoon liquid calcium chloride (if using pasteurized milk)
- 1/4 teaspoon liquid rennet diluted in 1/4 cup cool, chlorine-free water
- 1/4 cup cool, chlorine-free water
- Cheese salt or kosher salt
- Optional: annatto extract or powder for color (traditional for Muenster cheese)

Instructions:

1. Prepare Ingredients: Ensure all equipment is clean and sanitized. Dissolve the mesophilic starter culture in 1/4 cup of cool, non-chlorinated water. If using pasteurized milk, dissolve the liquid calcium chloride in the same amount of water. Prepare the liquid rennet and set it aside. If desired, mix a small amount of annatto extract or powder with water to create a solution for coloring the cheese.
2. Heat the Milk: Pour the 2 gallons of milk into a large, non-reactive pot. Warm the milk over medium heat to 90°F (32°C), stirring occasionally to prevent scorching.
3. Add Starter Culture: Once the milk reaches 90°F, remove it from the heat. Stir in the dissolved mesophilic starter culture (and calcium chloride, if using) with an up-and-down motion for about 30 seconds.
4. Add Annatto (Optional): If using annatto for coloring, gently stir in the annatto solution until the milk reaches your desired shade of orange. This step is optional but traditional for Muenster cheese.
5. Add the Rennet: Gently stir in the diluted rennet solution for about 30 seconds to distribute it evenly throughout the milk.
6. Let the Curds Form: Cover the pot and let it sit undisturbed at room temperature for about 45-60 minutes, or until you achieve a clean break. The curds should have set and separated from the whey.
7. Cut the Curds: Use a long knife to cut the curds into small, uniform pieces, about the size of peas.
8. Stir and Cook the Curds: Place the pot back on the stove and gently heat the curds over low heat, stirring gently to prevent sticking. Slowly raise the temperature to 100°F (38°C) over the course of 30 minutes, stirring frequently.
9. Drain the Whey: Line a large colander with cheesecloth and place it over a clean sink or a large bowl. Carefully ladle the curds into the colander to drain off the whey.
10. Salt the Curds: Transfer the drained curds into a large mixing bowl and sprinkle them with cheese salt or kosher salt. Gently toss the curds to distribute the salt evenly.

11. Mold the Cheese: Line cheese molds with cheesecloth and transfer the salted curds into them. Press the curds gently into the molds, smoothing the surface.
12. Press the Cheese: Place a follower or plate on top of the cheese in each mold and press them at a light pressure for 4-6 hours.
13. Age the Cheese: After pressing, transfer the cheeses to a cheese cave or refrigerator with a temperature of around 50-55°F (10-13°C) and high humidity. Age the cheese for at least 4-6 weeks, flipping them every few days to ensure even aging.
14. Enjoy: Your homemade Muenster cheese is now ready to be enjoyed! Slice it for sandwiches, melt it on burgers, or savor it on a cheese board with fruit and crackers. Enjoy the creamy texture and mild flavor of your homemade Muenster cheese!

Taleggio Cheese

Ingredients:

- 2 gallons whole milk (avoid ultra-pasteurized milk)
- 1/4 teaspoon mesophilic starter culture
- 1/4 teaspoon liquid calcium chloride (if using pasteurized milk)
- 1/4 teaspoon liquid rennet diluted in 1/4 cup cool, chlorine-free water
- 1/4 cup cool, chlorine-free water
- Cheese salt or kosher salt
- Penicillium candidum (white mold culture)
- Cheese ripening powder or salt (optional, for aging)

Instructions:

1. Prepare Ingredients: Ensure all equipment is clean and sanitized. Dissolve the mesophilic starter culture in 1/4 cup of cool, non-chlorinated water. If using pasteurized milk, dissolve the liquid calcium chloride in the same amount of water. Prepare the liquid rennet and set it aside. If available, prepare the Penicillium candidum culture according to the package instructions.
2. Heat the Milk: Pour the 2 gallons of milk into a large, non-reactive pot. Warm the milk over medium heat to 86°F (30°C), stirring occasionally to prevent scorching.
3. Add Starter Culture: Once the milk reaches 86°F, remove it from the heat. Stir in the dissolved mesophilic starter culture (and calcium chloride, if using) with an up-and-down motion for about 30 seconds.
4. Add the Rennet: Gently stir in the diluted rennet solution for about 30 seconds to distribute it evenly throughout the milk.
5. Let the Curds Form: Cover the pot and let it sit undisturbed at room temperature for about 45-60 minutes, or until you achieve a clean break. The curds should have set and separated from the whey.
6. Cut the Curds: Use a long knife to cut the curds into small, uniform pieces, about the size of peas.
7. Stir and Cook the Curds: Place the pot back on the stove and gently heat the curds over low heat, stirring gently to prevent sticking. Slowly raise the temperature to 100°F (38°C) over the course of 30 minutes, stirring frequently.
8. Drain the Whey: Line a large colander with cheesecloth and place it over a clean sink or a large bowl. Carefully ladle the curds into the colander to drain off the whey.

9. Salt the Curds: Transfer the drained curds into a large mixing bowl and sprinkle them with cheese salt or kosher salt. Gently toss the curds to distribute the salt evenly.
10. Prepare for Aging: Line cheese molds with cheesecloth and transfer the salted curds into them. Press the curds gently into the molds, smoothing the surface. If using, dust the surface of the cheese with cheese ripening powder or salt.
11. Inoculate with Mold: If using Penicillium candidum, spray or sprinkle a small amount onto the surface of the cheese and gently rub it in. This will encourage the growth of a white mold rind characteristic of Taleggio cheese.
12. Age the Cheese: Place the cheese molds on a cheese mat or rack in a cool, humid environment, ideally around 50-55°F (10-13°C) with high humidity. Let the cheese age for 4-6 weeks or longer, flipping it every few days to ensure even ripening. During aging, the cheese will develop its characteristic flavor and aroma.
13. Enjoy: Your homemade Taleggio cheese is now ready to be enjoyed! Serve it on a cheese board with crusty bread, fruit, and honey, or use it in your favorite recipes for a creamy, flavorful touch. Enjoy the unique taste and texture of your homemade Taleggio cheese!

Asiago Cheese

Ingredients:

- 2 gallons whole milk (avoid ultra-pasteurized milk)
- 1/4 teaspoon mesophilic starter culture
- 1/8 teaspoon liquid calcium chloride (if using pasteurized milk)
- 1/4 teaspoon liquid rennet diluted in 1/4 cup cool, chlorine-free water
- 1/4 cup cool, chlorine-free water
- Cheese salt or kosher salt

Instructions:

1. Prepare Ingredients: Ensure all equipment is clean and sanitized. Dissolve the mesophilic starter culture in 1/4 cup of cool, non-chlorinated water. If using pasteurized milk, dissolve the liquid calcium chloride in the same amount of water. Prepare the liquid rennet and set it aside.
2. Heat the Milk: Pour the 2 gallons of milk into a large, non-reactive pot. Warm the milk over medium heat to 90°F (32°C), stirring occasionally to prevent scorching.
3. Add Starter Culture: Once the milk reaches 90°F, remove it from the heat. Stir in the dissolved mesophilic starter culture (and calcium chloride, if using) with an up-and-down motion for about 30 seconds.
4. Add the Rennet: Gently stir in the diluted rennet solution for about 30 seconds to distribute it evenly throughout the milk.
5. Let the Curds Form: Cover the pot and let it sit undisturbed at room temperature for about 45-60 minutes, or until you achieve a clean break. The curds should have set and separated from the whey.
6. Cut the Curds: Use a long knife to cut the curds into small, uniform pieces, about the size of peas.
7. Stir and Cook the Curds: Place the pot back on the stove and gently heat the curds over low heat, stirring gently to prevent sticking. Slowly raise the temperature to 120°F (49°C) over the course of 30 minutes, stirring frequently.
8. Drain the Whey: Line a large colander with cheesecloth and place it over a clean sink or a large bowl. Carefully ladle the curds into the colander to drain off the whey.
9. Press the Curds: Transfer the drained curds into a cheese mold lined with cheesecloth. Press the curds at 20 pounds of pressure for 20 minutes. Then, remove the cheese from the mold, flip it, re-wrap it, and press it at 50 pounds of pressure for 12 hours.
10. Salt the Cheese: Remove the cheese from the mold and sprinkle both sides with cheese salt or kosher salt. Rub the salt gently into the surface of the cheese.
11. Age the Cheese: Place the salted cheese on a cheese mat or rack in a cool, humid environment, ideally around 50-55°F (10-13°C) with high humidity. Age the cheese for 3-6 months or longer, flipping it every few days and monitoring its progress.

12. Enjoy: Your homemade Asiago cheese is now ready to be enjoyed! Slice it for sandwiches, grate it over pasta, or savor it on a cheese board with crackers and fruit. Enjoy the nutty flavor and firm texture of your homemade Asiago cheese!

Ricotta Salata Cheese

Ingredients:

- 1 gallon whole milk (avoid ultra-pasteurized milk)
- 1/4 cup white vinegar or lemon juice
- Cheese salt or kosher salt

Instructions:

1. Heat the Milk: Pour the whole milk into a large, heavy-bottomed pot and heat it over medium heat until it reaches a temperature of around 200°F (93°C). Stir occasionally to prevent scorching.
2. Add Acid: Once the milk reaches the desired temperature, slowly pour in the white vinegar or lemon juice while stirring gently. Continue to heat the milk for a few more minutes until you see curds forming and the whey separating. If the whey remains cloudy, add a bit more vinegar or lemon juice.
3. Drain the Curds: Line a colander with cheesecloth and place it over a large bowl or in the sink. Carefully ladle or pour the curds into the cheesecloth-lined colander, allowing the whey to drain off. Let the curds drain for about 10-15 minutes.
4. Press the Cheese: After draining, gather the corners of the cheesecloth and tie them together to form a bundle. Hang the bundle over the sink or a bowl and let it drain for another 1-2 hours, or until the cheese reaches your desired consistency.
5. Salt the Cheese: Once the cheese has drained, remove it from the cheesecloth and transfer it to a clean surface. Sprinkle salt over the surface of the cheese and rub it gently to distribute the salt evenly.
6. Shape and Age (Optional): At this point, you can shape the cheese into a wheel or block by pressing it into a mold or wrapping it tightly in cheesecloth. If you prefer a firmer texture, you can age the cheese in the refrigerator for a few days to a week.
7. Enjoy: Your homemade Ricotta Salata cheese is now ready to be enjoyed! Serve it sliced or grated on salads, pasta dishes, or as part of a cheese platter. Enjoy the creamy texture and slightly salty flavor of your homemade Ricotta Salata cheese!

Pecorino Romano Cheese

Ingredients:

- 5 gallons sheep's milk
- 1/4 teaspoon thermophilic starter culture
- 1/4 teaspoon liquid rennet diluted in 1/4 cup cool, chlorine-free water
- 1/4 cup cool, chlorine-free water
- Cheese salt or kosher salt

Instructions:

1. Heat the Milk: Pour the sheep's milk into a large, non-reactive pot. Heat the milk slowly to 100°F (38°C) over low to medium heat, stirring occasionally to prevent scorching.
2. Add Starter Culture: Once the milk reaches 100°F, remove it from the heat. Stir in the thermophilic starter culture with an up-and-down motion for about 30 seconds.
3. Add the Rennet: Gently stir in the diluted rennet solution for about 30 seconds to distribute it evenly throughout the milk.
4. Let the Curds Form: Cover the pot and let it sit undisturbed at room temperature for about 30-45 minutes, or until you achieve a clean break. The curds should have set and separated from the whey.
5. Cut the Curds: Use a long knife to cut the curds into small, uniform pieces, about the size of peas.
6. Stir and Cook the Curds: Place the pot back on the stove and gently heat the curds over low heat, stirring gently to prevent sticking. Slowly raise the temperature to 122°F (50°C) over the course of 30 minutes, stirring frequently.
7. Drain the Whey: Line a large colander with cheesecloth and place it over a clean sink or a large bowl. Carefully ladle the curds into the colander to drain off the whey.
8. Salt the Curds: Transfer the drained curds into a large mixing bowl and sprinkle them with cheese salt or kosher salt. Gently toss the curds to distribute the salt evenly.
9. Mold the Cheese: Line cheese molds with cheesecloth and transfer the salted curds into them. Press the curds gently into the molds, smoothing the surface.
10. Press the Cheese: Place a follower or plate on top of the cheese in each mold and press them at a light pressure for 12 hours.
11. Air Dry and Salt Again: After pressing, remove the cheese from the molds and air dry it on a cheese mat or rack at room temperature for 1-2 days, or until the surface feels dry to the touch. Then, sprinkle salt on the surface of the cheese and rub it in gently.
12. Age the Cheese: Transfer the salted cheese to a cheese cave or refrigerator with a temperature of around 50-55°F (10-13°C) and moderate humidity. Age the cheese for at least 5-8 months, flipping it every few days and monitoring its progress.

13. Enjoy: Your homemade Pecorino Romano cheese is now ready to be enjoyed! Grate it over pasta, risotto, or soups, or enjoy it on its own with a glass of wine. Revel in the rich, salty flavor and firm texture of your homemade Pecorino Romano cheese!

Gruyère Cheese

Ingredients:

- 4 gallons whole milk (avoid ultra-pasteurized milk)
- 1/4 teaspoon mesophilic starter culture
- 1/4 teaspoon liquid calcium chloride (if using pasteurized milk)
- 1/4 teaspoon liquid rennet diluted in 1/4 cup cool, chlorine-free water
- 1/4 cup cool, chlorine-free water
- Cheese salt or kosher salt

Instructions:

1. Prepare Ingredients: Ensure all equipment is clean and sanitized. Dissolve the mesophilic starter culture in 1/4 cup of cool, non-chlorinated water. If using pasteurized milk, dissolve the liquid calcium chloride in the same amount of water. Prepare the liquid rennet and set it aside.
2. Heat the Milk: Pour the 4 gallons of milk into a large, non-reactive pot. Warm the milk over medium heat to 93°F (34°C), stirring occasionally to prevent scorching.
3. Add Starter Culture: Once the milk reaches 93°F, remove it from the heat. Stir in the dissolved mesophilic starter culture (and calcium chloride, if using) with an up-and-down motion for about 30 seconds.
4. Add the Rennet: Gently stir in the diluted rennet solution for about 30 seconds to distribute it evenly throughout the milk.
5. Let the Curds Form: Cover the pot and let it sit undisturbed at room temperature for about 40-50 minutes, or until you achieve a clean break. The curds should have set and separated from the whey.
6. Cut the Curds: Use a long knife to cut the curds into small, uniform pieces, about the size of peas.
7. Stir and Cook the Curds: Place the pot back on the stove and gently heat the curds over low heat, stirring gently to prevent sticking. Slowly raise the temperature to 122°F (50°C) over the course of 30 minutes, stirring frequently.
8. Drain the Whey: Line a large colander with cheesecloth and place it over a clean sink or a large bowl. Carefully ladle the curds into the colander to drain off the whey.
9. Salt the Curds: Transfer the drained curds into a large mixing bowl and sprinkle them with cheese salt or kosher salt. Gently toss the curds to distribute the salt evenly.

10. Mold the Cheese: Line cheese molds with cheesecloth and transfer the salted curds into them. Press the curds gently into the molds, smoothing the surface.
11. Press the Cheese: Place a follower or plate on top of the cheese in each mold and press them at a light pressure for 12 hours.
12. Brine the Cheese: After pressing, soak the cheese in a brine solution for 24-48 hours. The brine solution should be around 20-22% salt concentration.
13. Age the Cheese: Transfer the brined cheese to a cheese cave or refrigerator with a temperature of around 45-55°F (7-13°C) and high humidity. Age the cheese for at least 5-12 months, flipping it every few days and monitoring its progress.
14. Enjoy: Your homemade Gruyère cheese is now ready to be enjoyed! Slice it for sandwiches, melt it into fondue, or savor it on a cheese board with fruits and nuts. Revel in the nutty flavor and creamy texture of your homemade Gruyère cheese!

Roquefort Cheese

Ingredients:

- 2 gallons whole sheep's milk (cow's milk can be substituted)
- 1/4 teaspoon mesophilic starter culture
- 1/4 teaspoon Penicillium roqueforti mold powder
- 1/4 teaspoon liquid calcium chloride (if using pasteurized milk)
- 1/4 teaspoon liquid rennet diluted in 1/4 cup cool, chlorine-free water
- 1/4 cup cool, chlorine-free water
- Cheese salt or kosher salt

Instructions:

1. Prepare Ingredients: Ensure all equipment is clean and sanitized. Dissolve the mesophilic starter culture in 1/4 cup of cool, non-chlorinated water. Dissolve the Penicillium roqueforti mold powder in the same amount of water. If using pasteurized milk, dissolve the liquid calcium chloride in the same amount of water. Prepare the liquid rennet and set it aside.
2. Heat the Milk: Pour the 2 gallons of milk into a large, non-reactive pot. Warm the milk over medium heat to 86°F (30°C), stirring occasionally to prevent scorching.
3. Add Starter Culture: Once the milk reaches 86°F, remove it from the heat. Stir in the dissolved mesophilic starter culture and Penicillium roqueforti mold solution with an up-and-down motion for about 30 seconds.
4. Add the Rennet: Gently stir in the diluted rennet solution for about 30 seconds to distribute it evenly throughout the milk.
5. Let the Curds Form: Cover the pot and let it sit undisturbed at room temperature for about 45-60 minutes, or until you achieve a clean break. The curds should have set and separated from the whey.
6. Cut the Curds: Use a long knife to cut the curds into small, uniform pieces, about the size of peas.
7. Stir and Cook the Curds: Place the pot back on the stove and gently heat the curds over low heat, stirring gently to prevent sticking. Slowly raise the temperature to 100°F (38°C) over the course of 30 minutes, stirring frequently.
8. Drain the Whey: Line a large colander with cheesecloth and place it over a clean sink or a large bowl. Carefully ladle the curds into the colander to drain off the whey.
9. Salt the Curds: Transfer the drained curds into a large mixing bowl and sprinkle them with cheese salt or kosher salt. Gently toss the curds to distribute the salt evenly.
10. Mold the Cheese: Line cheese molds with cheesecloth and transfer the salted curds into them. Press the curds gently into the molds, smoothing the surface.
11. Press the Cheese: Place a follower or plate on top of the cheese in each mold and press them at a light pressure for 12 hours.

12. Pierce the Cheese: After pressing, use a skewer or knitting needle to pierce holes throughout the cheese to allow air to penetrate.
13. Age the Cheese: Transfer the pierced cheese to a cheese cave or refrigerator with a temperature of around 45-50°F (7-10°C) and high humidity. Age the cheese for at least 3-5 months, flipping it every few days and monitoring its progress.
14. Enjoy: Your homemade Roquefort cheese is now ready to be enjoyed! Serve it crumbled over salads, melted into sauces, or on a cheese board with fruit and crackers. Enjoy the tangy flavor and creamy texture of your homemade Roquefort cheese!

Raclette Cheese

Ingredients:

- 2 gallons whole cow's milk (preferably raw, but pasteurized milk can be used)
- 1/4 teaspoon thermophilic starter culture
- 1/4 teaspoon liquid calcium chloride (if using pasteurized milk)
- 1/4 teaspoon liquid rennet diluted in 1/4 cup cool, chlorine-free water
- 1/4 cup cool, chlorine-free water
- Cheese salt or kosher salt

Instructions:

1. Prepare Ingredients: Ensure all equipment is clean and sanitized. Dissolve the thermophilic starter culture in 1/4 cup of cool, non-chlorinated water. If using pasteurized milk, dissolve the liquid calcium chloride in the same amount of water. Prepare the liquid rennet and set it aside.
2. Heat the Milk: Pour the 2 gallons of milk into a large, non-reactive pot. Warm the milk over medium heat to 90°F (32°C), stirring occasionally to prevent scorching.
3. Add Starter Culture: Once the milk reaches 90°F, remove it from the heat. Stir in the dissolved thermophilic starter culture (and calcium chloride, if using) with an up-and-down motion for about 30 seconds.
4. Add the Rennet: Gently stir in the diluted rennet solution for about 30 seconds to distribute it evenly throughout the milk.
5. Let the Curds Form: Cover the pot and let it sit undisturbed at room temperature for about 30-40 minutes, or until you achieve a clean break. The curds should have set and separated from the whey.
6. Cut the Curds: Use a long knife to cut the curds into small, uniform pieces, about the size of peas.
7. Stir and Cook the Curds: Place the pot back on the stove and gently heat the curds over low heat, stirring gently to prevent sticking. Slowly raise the temperature to 126°F (52°C) over the course of 30 minutes, stirring frequently.
8. Drain the Whey: Line a large colander with cheesecloth and place it over a clean sink or a large bowl. Carefully ladle the curds into the colander to drain off the whey.
9. Salt the Curds: Transfer the drained curds into a large mixing bowl and sprinkle them with cheese salt or kosher salt. Gently toss the curds to distribute the salt evenly.
10. Mold the Cheese: Line cheese molds with cheesecloth and transfer the salted curds into them. Press the curds gently into the molds, smoothing the surface.
11. Press the Cheese: Place a follower or plate on top of the cheese in each mold and press them at a light pressure for 12 hours.

12. Age the Cheese: After pressing, transfer the cheese to a cheese cave or refrigerator with a temperature of around 50-55°F (10-13°C) and moderate humidity. Age the cheese for at least 3-4 months, flipping it every few days and monitoring its progress.
13. Enjoy: Your homemade Raclette cheese is now ready to be enjoyed! Melt it over potatoes or vegetables, or serve it on a cheese board with cured meats and crusty bread. Enjoy the creamy texture and rich flavor of your homemade Raclette cheese!

Stilton Cheese

Ingredients:

- 2 gallons whole cow's milk (preferably raw, but pasteurized milk can be used)
- 1/4 teaspoon mesophilic starter culture
- 1/4 teaspoon Penicillium roqueforti mold powder
- 1/4 teaspoon liquid calcium chloride (if using pasteurized milk)
- 1/4 teaspoon liquid rennet diluted in 1/4 cup cool, chlorine-free water
- 1/4 cup cool, chlorine-free water
- Cheese salt or kosher salt

Instructions:

1. Prepare Ingredients: Ensure all equipment is clean and sanitized. Dissolve the mesophilic starter culture in 1/4 cup of cool, non-chlorinated water. Dissolve the Penicillium roqueforti mold powder in the same amount of water. If using pasteurized milk, dissolve the liquid calcium chloride in the same amount of water. Prepare the liquid rennet and set it aside.
2. Heat the Milk: Pour the 2 gallons of milk into a large, non-reactive pot. Warm the milk over medium heat to 86°F (30°C), stirring occasionally to prevent scorching.
3. Add Starter Culture: Once the milk reaches 86°F, remove it from the heat. Stir in the dissolved mesophilic starter culture (and calcium chloride, if using) with an up-and-down motion for about 30 seconds.
4. Add the Rennet: Gently stir in the diluted rennet solution for about 30 seconds to distribute it evenly throughout the milk.
5. Add Mold Culture: Stir in the dissolved Penicillium roqueforti mold solution into the milk, making sure it's evenly distributed.
6. Let the Curds Form: Cover the pot and let it sit undisturbed at room temperature for about 45-60 minutes, or until you achieve a clean break. The curds should have set and separated from the whey.
7. Cut the Curds: Use a long knife to cut the curds into small, uniform pieces, about the size of peas.
8. Stir and Cook the Curds: Place the pot back on the stove and gently heat the curds over low heat, stirring gently to prevent sticking. Slowly raise the temperature to 102°F (39°C) over the course of 30 minutes, stirring frequently.

9. Drain the Whey: Line a large colander with cheesecloth and place it over a clean sink or a large bowl. Carefully ladle the curds into the colander to drain off the whey.
10. Salt the Curds: Transfer the drained curds into a large mixing bowl and sprinkle them with cheese salt or kosher salt. Gently toss the curds to distribute the salt evenly.
11. Mold the Cheese: Line cheese molds with cheesecloth and transfer the salted curds into them. Press the curds gently into the molds, smoothing the surface.
12. Press the Cheese: Place a follower or plate on top of the cheese in each mold and press them at a light pressure for 12 hours.
13. Age the Cheese: After pressing, transfer the cheese to a cheese cave or refrigerator with a temperature of around 50-55°F (10-13°C) and high humidity. Age the cheese for at least 8-12 weeks, flipping it every few days and monitoring its progress.
14. Enjoy: Your homemade Stilton cheese is now ready to be enjoyed! Serve it crumbled over salads, melted into sauces, or on a cheese board with fruit and crackers. Enjoy the rich flavor and creamy texture of your homemade Stilton cheese!

Gorgonzola Cheese

Ingredients:

- 2 gallons whole cow's milk (preferably raw, but pasteurized milk can be used)
- 1/4 teaspoon mesophilic starter culture
- 1/4 teaspoon Penicillium roqueforti mold powder
- 1/4 teaspoon liquid calcium chloride (if using pasteurized milk)
- 1/4 teaspoon liquid rennet diluted in 1/4 cup cool, chlorine-free water
- 1/4 cup cool, chlorine-free water
- Cheese salt or kosher salt

Instructions:

1. Prepare Ingredients: Ensure all equipment is clean and sanitized. Dissolve the mesophilic starter culture in 1/4 cup of cool, non-chlorinated water. Dissolve the Penicillium roqueforti mold powder in the same amount of water. If using pasteurized milk, dissolve the liquid calcium chloride in the same amount of water. Prepare the liquid rennet and set it aside.
2. Heat the Milk: Pour the 2 gallons of milk into a large, non-reactive pot. Warm the milk over medium heat to 86°F (30°C), stirring occasionally to prevent scorching.
3. Add Starter Culture: Once the milk reaches 86°F, remove it from the heat. Stir in the dissolved mesophilic starter culture (and calcium chloride, if using) with an up-and-down motion for about 30 seconds.
4. Add the Rennet: Gently stir in the diluted rennet solution for about 30 seconds to distribute it evenly throughout the milk.
5. Add Mold Culture: Stir in the dissolved Penicillium roqueforti mold solution into the milk, making sure it's evenly distributed.
6. Let the Curds Form: Cover the pot and let it sit undisturbed at room temperature for about 45-60 minutes, or until you achieve a clean break. The curds should have set and separated from the whey.
7. Cut the Curds: Use a long knife to cut the curds into small, uniform pieces, about the size of peas.
8. Stir and Cook the Curds: Place the pot back on the stove and gently heat the curds over low heat, stirring gently to prevent sticking. Slowly raise the temperature to 100°F (38°C) over the course of 30 minutes, stirring frequently.
9. Drain the Whey: Line a large colander with cheesecloth and place it over a clean sink or a large bowl. Carefully ladle the curds into the colander to drain off the whey.
10. Salt the Curds: Transfer the drained curds into a large mixing bowl and sprinkle them with cheese salt or kosher salt. Gently toss the curds to distribute the salt evenly.
11. Mold the Cheese: Line cheese molds with cheesecloth and transfer the salted curds into them. Press the curds gently into the molds, smoothing the surface.

12. Press the Cheese: Place a follower or plate on top of the cheese in each mold and press them at a light pressure for 12 hours.
13. Age the Cheese: After pressing, transfer the cheese to a cheese cave or refrigerator with a temperature of around 50-55°F (10-13°C) and high humidity. Age the cheese for at least 3-4 weeks, flipping it every few days and monitoring its progress.
14. Enjoy: Your homemade Gorgonzola cheese is now ready to be enjoyed! Serve it crumbled over salads, melted into sauces, or on a cheese board with fruit and crackers. Enjoy the creamy texture and rich flavor of your homemade Gorgonzola cheese!

Edam Cheese

Ingredients:

- 2 gallons whole cow's milk (preferably raw, but pasteurized milk can be used)
- 1/4 teaspoon mesophilic starter culture
- 1/4 teaspoon liquid calcium chloride (if using pasteurized milk)
- 1/4 teaspoon liquid rennet diluted in 1/4 cup cool, chlorine-free water
- 1/4 cup cool, chlorine-free water
- Cheese salt or kosher salt
- Annatto cheese coloring (optional)

Instructions:

1. Prepare Ingredients: Ensure all equipment is clean and sanitized. Dissolve the mesophilic starter culture in 1/4 cup of cool, non-chlorinated water. If using pasteurized milk, dissolve the liquid calcium chloride in the same amount of water. Prepare the liquid rennet and set it aside.
2. Heat the Milk: Pour the 2 gallons of milk into a large, non-reactive pot. Warm the milk over medium heat to 90°F (32°C), stirring occasionally to prevent scorching.
3. Add Starter Culture: Once the milk reaches 90°F, remove it from the heat. Stir in the dissolved mesophilic starter culture (and calcium chloride, if using) with an up-and-down motion for about 30 seconds.
4. Add Annatto (optional): If desired, add a few drops of annatto cheese coloring to achieve the characteristic yellow-orange color of Edam cheese. Stir well to distribute the coloring evenly.
5. Add the Rennet: Gently stir in the diluted rennet solution for about 30 seconds to distribute it evenly throughout the milk.
6. Let the Curds Form: Cover the pot and let it sit undisturbed at room temperature for about 45-60 minutes, or until you achieve a clean break. The curds should have set and separated from the whey.
7. Cut the Curds: Use a long knife to cut the curds into small, uniform pieces, about the size of peas.
8. Stir and Cook the Curds: Place the pot back on the stove and gently heat the curds over low heat, stirring gently to prevent sticking. Slowly raise the temperature to 102°F (39°C) over the course of 30 minutes, stirring frequently.
9. Drain the Whey: Line a large colander with cheesecloth and place it over a clean sink or a large bowl. Carefully ladle the curds into the colander to drain off the whey.
10. Press the Cheese: Transfer the drained curds into a cheese mold lined with cheesecloth. Press the curds at a light pressure for 1 hour.
11. Salt the Cheese: Remove the cheese from the mold and sprinkle both sides with cheese salt or kosher salt. Rub the salt gently into the surface of the cheese.

12. Age the Cheese: Transfer the salted cheese to a cheese cave or refrigerator with a temperature of around 50-55°F (10-13°C) and high humidity. Age the cheese for at least 4-6 weeks, flipping it every few days and monitoring its progress.
13. Enjoy: Your homemade Edam cheese is now ready to be enjoyed! Slice it for sandwiches, melt it on burgers, or enjoy it on a cheese platter with crackers and fruit. Revel in the creamy texture and mild flavor of your homemade Edam cheese!

Jarlsberg Cheese

Ingredients:

- 2 gallons whole cow's milk (preferably raw, but pasteurized milk can be used)
- 1/4 teaspoon mesophilic starter culture
- 1/4 teaspoon liquid calcium chloride (if using pasteurized milk)
- 1/4 teaspoon liquid rennet diluted in 1/4 cup cool, chlorine-free water
- 1/4 cup cool, chlorine-free water
- Cheese salt or kosher salt
- Propionic Shermanii culture (for the characteristic eyes in the cheese, optional)

Instructions:

1. Prepare Ingredients: Ensure all equipment is clean and sanitized. Dissolve the mesophilic starter culture in 1/4 cup of cool, non-chlorinated water. If using pasteurized milk, dissolve the liquid calcium chloride in the same amount of water. Prepare the liquid rennet and set it aside.
2. Heat the Milk: Pour the 2 gallons of milk into a large, non-reactive pot. Warm the milk over medium heat to 90°F (32°C), stirring occasionally to prevent scorching.
3. Add Starter Culture: Once the milk reaches 90°F, remove it from the heat. Stir in the dissolved mesophilic starter culture (and calcium chloride, if using) with an up-and-down motion for about 30 seconds.
4. Add Propionic Shermanii (optional): If you want the characteristic eyes in the cheese, you can add propionic shermanii culture at this stage. Follow the manufacturer's instructions for the amount to add.
5. Add the Rennet: Gently stir in the diluted rennet solution for about 30 seconds to distribute it evenly throughout the milk.
6. Let the Curds Form: Cover the pot and let it sit undisturbed at room temperature for about 45-60 minutes, or until you achieve a clean break. The curds should have set and separated from the whey.
7. Cut the Curds: Use a long knife to cut the curds into small, uniform pieces, about the size of peas.
8. Stir and Cook the Curds: Place the pot back on the stove and gently heat the curds over low heat, stirring gently to prevent sticking. Slowly raise the temperature to 120°F (49°C) over the course of 30 minutes, stirring frequently.
9. Drain the Whey: Line a large colander with cheesecloth and place it over a clean sink or a large bowl. Carefully ladle the curds into the colander to drain off the whey.
10. Salt the Curds: Transfer the drained curds into a large mixing bowl and sprinkle them with cheese salt or kosher salt. Gently toss the curds to distribute the salt evenly.
11. Mold the Cheese: Line cheese molds with cheesecloth and transfer the salted curds into them. Press the curds gently into the molds, smoothing the surface.

12. Press the Cheese: Place a follower or plate on top of the cheese in each mold and press them at a light pressure for 12 hours.
13. Age the Cheese: After pressing, transfer the cheese to a cheese cave or refrigerator with a temperature of around 50-55°F (10-13°C) and high humidity. Age the cheese for at least 3-6 weeks, flipping it every few days and monitoring its progress.
14. Enjoy: Your homemade Jarlsberg cheese is now ready to be enjoyed! Slice it for sandwiches, melt it on burgers, or enjoy it on a cheese platter with crackers and fruit. Revel in the creamy texture and mild, nutty flavor of your homemade Jarlsberg cheese!

Provolone Cheese

Ingredients:

- 2 gallons whole cow's milk (preferably raw, but pasteurized milk can be used)
- 1/4 teaspoon mesophilic starter culture
- 1/4 teaspoon liquid calcium chloride (if using pasteurized milk)
- 1/4 teaspoon liquid rennet diluted in 1/4 cup cool, chlorine-free water
- 1/4 cup cool, chlorine-free water
- Cheese salt or kosher salt
- Lipase powder (optional, for a sharper flavor)

Instructions:

1. Prepare Ingredients: Ensure all equipment is clean and sanitized. Dissolve the mesophilic starter culture in 1/4 cup of cool, non-chlorinated water. If using pasteurized milk, dissolve the liquid calcium chloride in the same amount of water. Prepare the liquid rennet and set it aside.
2. Heat the Milk: Pour the 2 gallons of milk into a large, non-reactive pot. Warm the milk over medium heat to 90°F (32°C), stirring occasionally to prevent scorching.
3. Add Starter Culture: Once the milk reaches 90°F, remove it from the heat. Stir in the dissolved mesophilic starter culture (and calcium chloride, if using) with an up-and-down motion for about 30 seconds.
4. Add Lipase (optional): If you want a sharper flavor, you can add lipase powder at this stage. Follow the manufacturer's instructions for the amount to add.
5. Add the Rennet: Gently stir in the diluted rennet solution for about 30 seconds to distribute it evenly throughout the milk.
6. Let the Curds Form: Cover the pot and let it sit undisturbed at room temperature for about 45-60 minutes, or until you achieve a clean break. The curds should have set and separated from the whey.
7. Cut the Curds: Use a long knife to cut the curds into small, uniform pieces, about the size of peas.
8. Stir and Cook the Curds: Place the pot back on the stove and gently heat the curds over low heat, stirring gently to prevent sticking. Slowly raise the temperature to 118°F (48°C) over the course of 30 minutes, stirring frequently.
9. Drain the Whey: Line a large colander with cheesecloth and place it over a clean sink or a large bowl. Carefully ladle the curds into the colander to drain off the whey.
10. Salt the Curds: Transfer the drained curds into a large mixing bowl and sprinkle them with cheese salt or kosher salt. Gently toss the curds to distribute the salt evenly.
11. Mold the Cheese: Line cheese molds with cheesecloth and transfer the salted curds into them. Press the curds gently into the molds, smoothing the surface.

12. Press the Cheese: Place a follower or plate on top of the cheese in each mold and press them at a light pressure for 12 hours.
13. Age the Cheese: After pressing, transfer the cheese to a cheese cave or refrigerator with a temperature of around 55-60°F (13-16°C) and moderate humidity. Age the cheese for at least 2-3 months, flipping it every few days and monitoring its progress.
14. Enjoy: Your homemade Provolone cheese is now ready to be enjoyed! Slice it for sandwiches, melt it over pasta dishes, or enjoy it on a cheese platter with olives and crusty bread. Revel in the creamy texture and mild, tangy flavor of your homemade Provolone cheese!

Burrata Cheese

Ingredients:

- 2 gallons whole cow's milk (preferably raw, but pasteurized milk can be used)
- 1/4 teaspoon mesophilic starter culture
- 1/4 teaspoon liquid calcium chloride (if using pasteurized milk)
- 1/4 teaspoon liquid rennet diluted in 1/4 cup cool, chlorine-free water
- 1/4 cup cool, chlorine-free water
- Cheese salt or kosher salt
- Fresh cream (for the filling)

Instructions:

1. Prepare Ingredients: Ensure all equipment is clean and sanitized. Dissolve the mesophilic starter culture in 1/4 cup of cool, non-chlorinated water. If using pasteurized milk, dissolve the liquid calcium chloride in the same amount of water. Prepare the liquid rennet and set it aside.
2. Heat the Milk: Pour the 2 gallons of milk into a large, non-reactive pot. Warm the milk over medium heat to 90°F (32°C), stirring occasionally to prevent scorching.
3. Add Starter Culture: Once the milk reaches 90°F, remove it from the heat. Stir in the dissolved mesophilic starter culture (and calcium chloride, if using) with an up-and-down motion for about 30 seconds.
4. Add the Rennet: Gently stir in the diluted rennet solution for about 30 seconds to distribute it evenly throughout the milk.
5. Let the Curds Form: Cover the pot and let it sit undisturbed at room temperature for about 45-60 minutes, or until you achieve a clean break. The curds should have set and separated from the whey.
6. Cut the Curds: Use a long knife to cut the curds into small, uniform pieces, about the size of peas.
7. Stir and Cook the Curds: Place the pot back on the stove and gently heat the curds over low heat, stirring gently to prevent sticking. Slowly raise the temperature to 105°F (40°C) over the course of 30 minutes, stirring frequently.
8. Drain the Whey: Line a large colander with cheesecloth and place it over a clean sink or a large bowl. Carefully ladle the curds into the colander to drain off the whey. Reserve some whey for stretching the cheese later.
9. Stretch the Curds: Transfer the drained curds to a large bowl and pour some of the reserved whey over them. Working quickly, knead and stretch the curds like you would for mozzarella until they become smooth and elastic.
10. Form the Burrata: Take a portion of the stretched curds and flatten it into a disc. Place a spoonful of fresh cream in the center, then gather the edges of the curds and pinch them closed to seal in the cream. Shape it into a round ball.

11. Salt the Burrata: Sprinkle the formed Burrata with cheese salt or kosher salt to taste.
12. Serve or Store: Your homemade Burrata cheese is now ready to be enjoyed! Serve it fresh with tomatoes, basil, and a drizzle of olive oil, or store it in the refrigerator submerged in whey for up to a few days.

Making Burrata cheese requires some practice, especially in the stretching and forming process. But with patience and attention to detail, you can create delicious, creamy Burrata cheese at home.

Quark Cheese

Ingredients:

- 1 gallon whole cow's milk (preferably fresh and not ultra-pasteurized)
- 1/4 cup cultured buttermilk or mesophilic starter culture
- Cheese salt or kosher salt (optional)

Instructions:

1. Heat the Milk: Pour the milk into a large, non-reactive pot and heat it over medium-low heat, stirring frequently to prevent scorching. Heat the milk until it reaches around 185°F (85°C).
2. Cool the Milk: Once the milk reaches the desired temperature, remove it from the heat and allow it to cool to around 72-77°F (22-25°C). You can speed up this process by placing the pot in an ice water bath.
3. Add the Culture: Once the milk has cooled, add the cultured buttermilk or mesophilic starter culture. Stir well to ensure the culture is evenly distributed throughout the milk.
4. Incubate the Milk: Cover the pot with a lid and let it sit at room temperature for about 12-24 hours. During this time, the milk will ferment and thicken into Quark.
5. Check for Coagulation: After the incubation period, check to see if the milk has coagulated into a custard-like consistency. It should have thickened considerably and formed curds.
6. Drain the Whey: Line a colander with cheesecloth or a clean kitchen towel and place it over a large bowl or sink. Carefully ladle the thickened milk (curds) into the cheesecloth-lined colander to separate the curds from the whey.
7. Drain Further (Optional): If you desire a thicker Quark, you can gather the corners of the cheesecloth and tie them together to form a bag. Hang the bag over a bowl or sink and allow the whey to drain for several hours or overnight in the refrigerator.
8. Salt (Optional): Once the Quark reaches your desired consistency, you can add salt to taste, if desired.
9. Store: Transfer the Quark to a clean container with a lid and store it in the refrigerator. It will keep for about a week.
10. Enjoy: Your homemade Quark cheese is now ready to be enjoyed! Use it as a spread on bread or toast, mix it into dips and sauces, or use it in recipes that call for soft cheese.

Making Quark cheese at home is a simple and rewarding process, and you can customize it to suit your taste preferences.

Tilsit Cheese

Ingredients:

- 2 gallons whole cow's milk (preferably raw, but pasteurized milk can be used)
- 1/4 teaspoon mesophilic starter culture
- 1/4 teaspoon liquid calcium chloride (if using pasteurized milk)
- 1/4 teaspoon liquid rennet diluted in 1/4 cup cool, chlorine-free water
- 1/4 cup cool, chlorine-free water
- Cheese salt or kosher salt
- Propionic Shermanii culture (optional, for characteristic eyes in the cheese)

Instructions:

1. Prepare Ingredients: Ensure all equipment is clean and sanitized. Dissolve the mesophilic starter culture in 1/4 cup of cool, non-chlorinated water. If using pasteurized milk, dissolve the liquid calcium chloride in the same amount of water. Prepare the liquid rennet and set it aside.
2. Heat the Milk: Pour the 2 gallons of milk into a large, non-reactive pot. Warm the milk over medium heat to 90°F (32°C), stirring occasionally to prevent scorching.
3. Add Starter Culture: Once the milk reaches 90°F, remove it from the heat. Stir in the dissolved mesophilic starter culture (and calcium chloride, if using) with an up-and-down motion for about 30 seconds.
4. Add Propionic Shermanii (optional): If you want the characteristic eyes in the cheese, you can add propionic shermanii culture at this stage. Follow the manufacturer's instructions for the amount to add.
5. Add the Rennet: Gently stir in the diluted rennet solution for about 30 seconds to distribute it evenly throughout the milk.
6. Let the Curds Form: Cover the pot and let it sit undisturbed at room temperature for about 45-60 minutes, or until you achieve a clean break. The curds should have set and separated from the whey.
7. Cut the Curds: Use a long knife to cut the curds into small, uniform pieces, about the size of peas.
8. Stir and Cook the Curds: Place the pot back on the stove and gently heat the curds over low heat, stirring gently to prevent sticking. Slowly raise the temperature to 118°F (48°C) over the course of 30 minutes, stirring frequently.
9. Drain the Whey: Line a large colander with cheesecloth and place it over a clean sink or a large bowl. Carefully ladle the curds into the colander to drain off the whey.
10. Salt the Curds: Transfer the drained curds into a large mixing bowl and sprinkle them with cheese salt or kosher salt. Gently toss the curds to distribute the salt evenly.
11. Mold the Cheese: Line cheese molds with cheesecloth and transfer the salted curds into them. Press the curds gently into the molds, smoothing the surface.

12. Press the Cheese: Place a follower or plate on top of the cheese in each mold and press them at a light pressure for 12 hours.
13. Age the Cheese: After pressing, transfer the cheese to a cheese cave or refrigerator with a temperature of around 50-55°F (10-13°C) and high humidity. Age the cheese for at least 2-3 months, flipping it every few days and monitoring its progress.
14. Enjoy: Your homemade Tilsit cheese is now ready to be enjoyed! Slice it for sandwiches, melt it on burgers, or enjoy it on a cheese platter with fruit and crackers. Revel in the creamy texture and slightly pungent flavor of your homemade Tilsit cheese!

Fromage Blanc Cheese

Ingredients:

- 1 gallon whole cow's milk (preferably fresh and not ultra-pasteurized)
- 1/4 cup cultured buttermilk or mesophilic starter culture
- Cheese salt or kosher salt (optional)

Instructions:

1. Heat the Milk: Pour the milk into a large, non-reactive pot and heat it over medium-low heat, stirring frequently to prevent scorching. Heat the milk until it reaches around 180°F (82°C).
2. Cool the Milk: Once the milk reaches the desired temperature, remove it from the heat and allow it to cool to around 72-77°F (22-25°C). You can speed up this process by placing the pot in an ice water bath.
3. Add the Culture: Once the milk has cooled, add the cultured buttermilk or mesophilic starter culture. Stir well to ensure the culture is evenly distributed throughout the milk.
4. Incubate the Milk: Cover the pot with a lid and let it sit at room temperature for about 12-24 hours. During this time, the milk will ferment and thicken into Fromage Blanc.
5. Check for Coagulation: After the incubation period, check to see if the milk has coagulated into a thickened, custard-like consistency. It should have thickened considerably and formed curds.
6. Drain the Whey: Line a colander with cheesecloth or a clean kitchen towel and place it over a large bowl or sink. Carefully ladle the thickened milk (curds) into the cheesecloth-lined colander to separate the curds from the whey.
7. Drain Further (Optional): If you desire a thicker Fromage Blanc, you can gather the corners of the cheesecloth and tie them together to form a bag. Hang the bag over a bowl or sink and allow the whey to drain for several hours or overnight in the refrigerator.
8. Salt (Optional): Once the Fromage Blanc reaches your desired consistency, you can add salt to taste, if desired.
9. Store: Transfer the Fromage Blanc to a clean container with a lid and store it in the refrigerator. It will keep for about a week.
10. Enjoy: Your homemade Fromage Blanc cheese is now ready to be enjoyed! Use it as a spread on bread or toast, mix it into dips and sauces, or use it in recipes that call for soft cheese.

Making Fromage Blanc cheese at home is a simple and rewarding process, and you can customize it to suit your taste preferences.

Reblochon Cheese

Ingredients:

- 2 gallons whole cow's milk (preferably raw, but pasteurized milk can be used)
- 1/4 teaspoon mesophilic starter culture
- 1/4 teaspoon liquid calcium chloride (if using pasteurized milk)
- 1/4 teaspoon liquid rennet diluted in 1/4 cup cool, chlorine-free water
- 1/4 cup cool, chlorine-free water
- Cheese salt or kosher salt
- Propionic Shermanii culture (optional, for the characteristic eyes in the cheese)

Instructions:

1. Prepare Ingredients: Ensure all equipment is clean and sanitized. Dissolve the mesophilic starter culture in 1/4 cup of cool, non-chlorinated water. If using pasteurized milk, dissolve the liquid calcium chloride in the same amount of water. Prepare the liquid rennet and set it aside.
2. Heat the Milk: Pour the 2 gallons of milk into a large, non-reactive pot. Warm the milk over medium heat to 90°F (32°C), stirring occasionally to prevent scorching.
3. Add Starter Culture: Once the milk reaches 90°F, remove it from the heat. Stir in the dissolved mesophilic starter culture (and calcium chloride, if using) with an up-and-down motion for about 30 seconds.
4. Add Propionic Shermanii (optional): If you want the characteristic eyes in the cheese, you can add propionic shermanii culture at this stage. Follow the manufacturer's instructions for the amount to add.
5. Add the Rennet: Gently stir in the diluted rennet solution for about 30 seconds to distribute it evenly throughout the milk.
6. Let the Curds Form: Cover the pot and let it sit undisturbed at room temperature for about 45-60 minutes, or until you achieve a clean break. The curds should have set and separated from the whey.
7. Cut the Curds: Use a long knife to cut the curds into small, uniform pieces, about the size of peas.
8. Stir and Cook the Curds: Place the pot back on the stove and gently heat the curds over low heat, stirring gently to prevent sticking. Slowly raise the temperature to 126°F (52°C) over the course of 30 minutes, stirring frequently.
9. Drain the Whey: Line a large colander with cheesecloth and place it over a clean sink or a large bowl. Carefully ladle the curds into the colander to drain off the whey.
10. Salt the Curds: Transfer the drained curds into a large mixing bowl and sprinkle them with cheese salt or kosher salt. Gently toss the curds to distribute the salt evenly.
11. Mold the Cheese: Line cheese molds with cheesecloth and transfer the salted curds into them. Press the curds gently into the molds, smoothing the surface.

12. Press the Cheese: Place a follower or plate on top of the cheese in each mold and press them at a light pressure for 12 hours.
13. Age the Cheese: After pressing, transfer the cheese to a cheese cave or refrigerator with a temperature of around 48-52°F (9-11°C) and high humidity. Age the cheese for at least 3-4 weeks, flipping it every few days and monitoring its progress.
14. Enjoy: Your homemade Reblochon cheese is now ready to be enjoyed! Serve it melted on potatoes or in traditional tartiflette, or enjoy it on a cheese platter with crusty bread and charcuterie. Revel in the creamy texture and earthy flavor of your homemade Reblochon cheese!

Red Leicester Cheese

Ingredients:

- 2 gallons whole cow's milk (preferably raw, but pasteurized milk can be used)
- 1/4 teaspoon mesophilic starter culture
- 1/4 teaspoon liquid calcium chloride (if using pasteurized milk)
- 1/4 teaspoon liquid annatto coloring (for the characteristic orange color)
- 1/4 teaspoon liquid rennet diluted in 1/4 cup cool, chlorine-free water
- 1/4 cup cool, chlorine-free water
- Cheese salt or kosher salt

Instructions:

1. Prepare Ingredients: Ensure all equipment is clean and sanitized. Dissolve the mesophilic starter culture in 1/4 cup of cool, non-chlorinated water. If using pasteurized milk, dissolve the liquid calcium chloride in the same amount of water. Prepare the liquid rennet and annatto coloring, if using, and set them aside.
2. Heat the Milk: Pour the 2 gallons of milk into a large, non-reactive pot. Warm the milk over medium heat to 86°F (30°C), stirring occasionally to prevent scorching.
3. Add Starter Culture: Once the milk reaches 86°F, remove it from the heat. Stir in the dissolved mesophilic starter culture (and calcium chloride, if using) with an up-and-down motion for about 30 seconds.
4. Add Annatto Coloring: Stir in the liquid annatto coloring to achieve the desired orange color for Red Leicester cheese. Stir well to distribute the coloring evenly.
5. Add the Rennet: Gently stir in the diluted rennet solution for about 30 seconds to distribute it evenly throughout the milk.
6. Let the Curds Form: Cover the pot and let it sit undisturbed at room temperature for about 45-60 minutes, or until you achieve a clean break. The curds should have set and separated from the whey.
7. Cut the Curds: Use a long knife to cut the curds into small, uniform pieces, about the size of peas.
8. Stir and Cook the Curds: Place the pot back on the stove and gently heat the curds over low heat, stirring gently to prevent sticking. Slowly raise the temperature to 102°F (39°C) over the course of 30 minutes, stirring frequently.
9. Drain the Whey: Line a large colander with cheesecloth and place it over a clean sink or a large bowl. Carefully ladle the curds into the colander to drain off the whey.
10. Press the Cheese: Transfer the drained curds into a cheese mold lined with cheesecloth. Press the curds at a light pressure for 1 hour.
11. Salt the Cheese: Remove the cheese from the mold and sprinkle both sides with cheese salt or kosher salt. Rub the salt gently into the surface of the cheese.

12. Age the Cheese: Transfer the salted cheese to a cheese cave or refrigerator with a temperature of around 50-55°F (10-13°C) and moderate humidity. Age the cheese for at least 2-3 months, flipping it every few days and monitoring its progress.
13. Enjoy: Your homemade Red Leicester cheese is now ready to be enjoyed! Slice it for sandwiches, grate it for melting over dishes, or enjoy it on a cheese platter with fruit and crackers. Revel in the creamy texture and slightly nutty flavor of your homemade Red Leicester cheese!

Wensleydale Cheese

Ingredients:

- 2 gallons whole cow's milk (preferably raw, but pasteurized milk can be used)
- 1/4 teaspoon mesophilic starter culture
- 1/4 teaspoon liquid calcium chloride (if using pasteurized milk)
- 1/4 teaspoon liquid rennet diluted in 1/4 cup cool, chlorine-free water
- 1/4 cup cool, chlorine-free water
- Cheese salt or kosher salt
- Optional: dried cranberries or other fruit for flavor variation

Instructions:

1. Prepare Ingredients: Ensure all equipment is clean and sanitized. Dissolve the mesophilic starter culture in 1/4 cup of cool, non-chlorinated water. If using pasteurized milk, dissolve the liquid calcium chloride in the same amount of water. Prepare the liquid rennet and set it aside.
2. Heat the Milk: Pour the 2 gallons of milk into a large, non-reactive pot. Warm the milk over medium heat to 86°F (30°C), stirring occasionally to prevent scorching.
3. Add Starter Culture: Once the milk reaches 86°F, remove it from the heat. Stir in the dissolved mesophilic starter culture (and calcium chloride, if using) with an up-and-down motion for about 30 seconds.
4. Add the Rennet: Gently stir in the diluted rennet solution for about 30 seconds to distribute it evenly throughout the milk.
5. Let the Curds Form: Cover the pot and let it sit undisturbed at room temperature for about 45-60 minutes, or until you achieve a clean break. The curds should have set and separated from the whey.
6. Cut the Curds: Use a long knife to cut the curds into small, uniform pieces, about the size of peas.
7. Stir and Cook the Curds: Place the pot back on the stove and gently heat the curds over low heat, stirring gently to prevent sticking. Slowly raise the temperature to 102°F (39°C) over the course of 30 minutes, stirring frequently.
8. Drain the Whey: Line a large colander with cheesecloth and place it over a clean sink or a large bowl. Carefully ladle the curds into the colander to drain off the whey.
9. Optional: Add Fruit: If you want to add fruit to your Wensleydale cheese, mix in dried cranberries or other fruit at this stage.
10. Mold the Cheese: Line cheese molds with cheesecloth and transfer the drained curds into them. Press the curds gently into the molds, smoothing the surface.
11. Press the Cheese: Place a follower or plate on top of the cheese in each mold and press them at a light pressure for 12 hours.

12. Salt the Cheese: Remove the cheese from the molds and sprinkle both sides with cheese salt or kosher salt. Rub the salt gently into the surface of the cheese.
13. Age the Cheese: Transfer the salted cheese to a cheese cave or refrigerator with a temperature of around 50-55°F (10-13°C) and moderate humidity. Age the cheese for at least 4-6 weeks, flipping it every few days and monitoring its progress.
14. Enjoy: Your homemade Wensleydale cheese is now ready to be enjoyed! Slice it for sandwiches, crumble it over salads, or enjoy it on a cheese platter with crackers and fruit. Revel in the creamy texture and mild, tangy flavor of your homemade Wensleydale cheese!

Double Gloucester Cheese

Ingredients:

- 2 gallons whole cow's milk (preferably raw, but pasteurized milk can be used)
- 1/4 teaspoon mesophilic starter culture
- 1/4 teaspoon liquid calcium chloride (if using pasteurized milk)
- 1/4 teaspoon liquid annatto coloring (for the characteristic orange color)
- 1/4 teaspoon liquid rennet diluted in 1/4 cup cool, chlorine-free water
- 1/4 cup cool, chlorine-free water
- Cheese salt or kosher salt

Instructions:

1. Prepare Ingredients: Ensure all equipment is clean and sanitized. Dissolve the mesophilic starter culture in 1/4 cup of cool, non-chlorinated water. If using pasteurized milk, dissolve the liquid calcium chloride in the same amount of water. Prepare the liquid rennet and annatto coloring, if using, and set them aside.
2. Heat the Milk: Pour the 2 gallons of milk into a large, non-reactive pot. Warm the milk over medium heat to 86°F (30°C), stirring occasionally to prevent scorching.
3. Add Starter Culture: Once the milk reaches 86°F, remove it from the heat. Stir in the dissolved mesophilic starter culture (and calcium chloride, if using) with an up-and-down motion for about 30 seconds.
4. Add Annatto Coloring: Stir in the liquid annatto coloring to achieve the desired orange color for Double Gloucester cheese. Stir well to distribute the coloring evenly.
5. Add the Rennet: Gently stir in the diluted rennet solution for about 30 seconds to distribute it evenly throughout the milk.
6. Let the Curds Form: Cover the pot and let it sit undisturbed at room temperature for about 45-60 minutes, or until you achieve a clean break. The curds should have set and separated from the whey.
7. Cut the Curds: Use a long knife to cut the curds into small, uniform pieces, about the size of peas.
8. Stir and Cook the Curds: Place the pot back on the stove and gently heat the curds over low heat, stirring gently to prevent sticking. Slowly raise the temperature to 102°F (39°C) over the course of 30 minutes, stirring frequently.
9. Drain the Whey: Line a large colander with cheesecloth and place it over a clean sink or a large bowl. Carefully ladle the curds into the colander to drain off the whey.
10. Press the Cheese: Transfer the drained curds into a cheese mold lined with cheesecloth. Press the curds at a light pressure for 1 hour.
11. Salt the Cheese: Remove the cheese from the mold and sprinkle both sides with cheese salt or kosher salt. Rub the salt gently into the surface of the cheese.

12. Age the Cheese: Transfer the salted cheese to a cheese cave or refrigerator with a temperature of around 50-55°F (10-13°C) and moderate humidity. Age the cheese for at least 3-6 months, flipping it every few days and monitoring its progress.
13. Enjoy: Your homemade Double Gloucester cheese is now ready to be enjoyed! Slice it for sandwiches, shred it for melting over dishes, or enjoy it on a cheese platter with fruit and crackers. Revel in the creamy texture and slightly tangy flavor of your homemade Double Gloucester cheese!

Saint André Cheese

Ingredients:

- 1 gallon whole cow's milk (preferably pasteurized)
- 1 quart heavy cream
- Mesophilic starter culture
- Liquid rennet
- Cheese salt or kosher salt

Instructions:

1. Heat the Milk: Pour the milk and heavy cream into a large, non-reactive pot. Heat the mixture over medium heat to 86°F (30°C), stirring occasionally to prevent scorching.
2. Add Starter Culture: Once the milk reaches 86°F, remove it from the heat. Stir in the mesophilic starter culture according to the package instructions.
3. Add Rennet: Dissolve the liquid rennet in a small amount of cool, chlorine-free water. Gently stir the rennet mixture into the milk.
4. Let the Curds Form: Cover the pot and let it sit undisturbed at room temperature for about 12-24 hours, or until the curds have formed and separated from the whey.
5. Cut and Drain the Curds: Cut the curds into small cubes and ladle them into cheese molds lined with cheesecloth. Let the curds drain for several hours or overnight, until they reach the desired consistency.
6. Salt the Cheese: Once the curds have drained, remove them from the molds and sprinkle them with cheese salt or kosher salt. Rub the salt gently into the surface of the cheese.
7. Age the Cheese: Transfer the salted cheese to a cheese cave or refrigerator with a temperature of around 50-55°F (10-13°C) and high humidity. Age the cheese for at least 2-4 weeks, flipping it every few days and monitoring its progress.
8. Enjoy: Your homemade triple-cream cheese is now ready to be enjoyed! Serve it on a cheese platter with fruit and crackers, or use it as a luxurious addition to sandwiches and salads. Revel in the rich and creamy texture of your homemade cheese creation!

Pont-l'Évêque Cheese

Ingredients:

- 2 gallons whole cow's milk (preferably raw, but pasteurized milk can be used)
- 1/4 teaspoon mesophilic starter culture
- 1/4 teaspoon liquid calcium chloride (if using pasteurized milk)
- 1/4 teaspoon liquid rennet diluted in 1/4 cup cool, chlorine-free water
- 1/4 cup cool, chlorine-free water
- Cheese salt or kosher salt

Instructions:

1. Prepare Ingredients: Ensure all equipment is clean and sanitized. Dissolve the mesophilic starter culture in 1/4 cup of cool, non-chlorinated water. If using pasteurized milk, dissolve the liquid calcium chloride in the same amount of water. Prepare the liquid rennet and set it aside.
2. Heat the Milk: Pour the 2 gallons of milk into a large, non-reactive pot. Warm the milk over medium heat to 86°F (30°C), stirring occasionally to prevent scorching.
3. Add Starter Culture: Once the milk reaches 86°F, remove it from the heat. Stir in the dissolved mesophilic starter culture (and calcium chloride, if using) with an up-and-down motion for about 30 seconds.
4. Add the Rennet: Gently stir in the diluted rennet solution for about 30 seconds to distribute it evenly throughout the milk.
5. Let the Curds Form: Cover the pot and let it sit undisturbed at room temperature for about 45-60 minutes, or until you achieve a clean break. The curds should have set and separated from the whey.
6. Cut the Curds: Use a long knife to cut the curds into small, uniform pieces, about the size of peas.
7. Stir and Cook the Curds: Place the pot back on the stove and gently heat the curds over low heat, stirring gently to prevent sticking. Slowly raise the temperature to 102°F (39°C) over the course of 30 minutes, stirring frequently.
8. Drain the Whey: Line a large colander with cheesecloth and place it over a clean sink or a large bowl. Carefully ladle the curds into the colander to drain off the whey.
9. Salt the Curds: Transfer the drained curds into a large mixing bowl and sprinkle them with cheese salt or kosher salt. Gently toss the curds to distribute the salt evenly.
10. Mold the Cheese: Line cheese molds with cheesecloth and transfer the salted curds into them. Press the curds gently into the molds, smoothing the surface.
11. Press the Cheese: Place a follower or plate on top of the cheese in each mold and press them at a light pressure for 12 hours.

12. Age the Cheese: After pressing, transfer the cheese to a cheese cave or refrigerator with a temperature of around 50-55°F (10-13°C) and moderate humidity. Age the cheese for at least 4-6 weeks, flipping it every few days and monitoring its progress.
13. Enjoy: Your homemade Pont-l'Évêque-style cheese is now ready to be enjoyed! Slice it for sandwiches, melt it on gratins, or enjoy it on a cheese platter with fruit and bread. Revel in the creamy texture and nuanced flavor of your homemade cheese!

Cambozola Cheese

Ingredients:

- 1 gallon whole cow's milk (preferably raw, but pasteurized milk can be used)
- 1/4 teaspoon mesophilic starter culture
- 1/4 teaspoon liquid calcium chloride (if using pasteurized milk)
- 1/8 teaspoon Penicillium roqueforti mold powder (for blue cheese characteristics)
- 1/4 teaspoon liquid rennet diluted in 1/4 cup cool, chlorine-free water
- 1/4 cup cool, chlorine-free water
- Cheese salt or kosher salt

Instructions:

1. Prepare Ingredients: Ensure all equipment is clean and sanitized. Dissolve the mesophilic starter culture in 1/4 cup of cool, non-chlorinated water. If using pasteurized milk, dissolve the liquid calcium chloride in the same amount of water. Prepare the liquid rennet and Penicillium roqueforti mold powder and set them aside.
2. Heat the Milk: Pour the 1 gallon of milk into a large, non-reactive pot. Warm the milk over medium heat to 86°F (30°C), stirring occasionally to prevent scorching.
3. Add Starter Culture and Mold: Once the milk reaches 86°F, remove it from the heat. Stir in the dissolved mesophilic starter culture (and calcium chloride, if using) with an up-and-down motion for about 30 seconds. Then add the Penicillium roqueforti mold powder and stir well to distribute it evenly throughout the milk.
4. Add the Rennet: Gently stir in the diluted rennet solution for about 30 seconds to distribute it evenly throughout the milk.
5. Let the Curds Form: Cover the pot and let it sit undisturbed at room temperature for about 45-60 minutes, or until you achieve a clean break. The curds should have set and separated from the whey.
6. Cut the Curds: Use a long knife to cut the curds into small, uniform pieces, about the size of peas.
7. Stir and Cook the Curds: Place the pot back on the stove and gently heat the curds over low heat, stirring gently to prevent sticking. Slowly raise the temperature to 102°F (39°C) over the course of 30 minutes, stirring frequently.
8. Drain the Whey: Line a large colander with cheesecloth and place it over a clean sink or a large bowl. Carefully ladle the curds into the colander to drain off the whey.
9. Salt the Curds: Transfer the drained curds into a large mixing bowl and sprinkle them with cheese salt or kosher salt. Gently toss the curds to distribute the salt evenly.
10. Mold the Cheese: Line cheese molds with cheesecloth and transfer the salted curds into them. Press the curds gently into the molds, smoothing the surface.
11. Press the Cheese: Place a follower or plate on top of the cheese in each mold and press them at a light pressure for 12 hours.

12. Age the Cheese: After pressing, transfer the cheese to a cheese cave or refrigerator with a temperature of around 50-55°F (10-13°C) and moderate humidity. Age the cheese for at least 4-6 weeks, flipping it every few days and monitoring its progress.
13. Enjoy: Your homemade Cambozola-style cheese is now ready to be enjoyed! Serve it on a cheese platter with crackers, nuts, and honey, or use it in sandwiches and salads. Revel in the creamy texture and rich flavor of your homemade cheese!

Red Windsor Cheese

Ingredients:

- 2 gallons whole cow's milk (preferably raw, but pasteurized milk can be used)
- 1/4 teaspoon mesophilic starter culture
- 1/4 teaspoon liquid calcium chloride (if using pasteurized milk)
- 1/4 teaspoon liquid annatto coloring (for the characteristic red-orange hue)
- 1/4 teaspoon liquid rennet diluted in 1/4 cup cool, chlorine-free water
- 1/4 cup cool, chlorine-free water
- Cheese salt or kosher salt

Instructions:

1. Prepare Ingredients: Ensure all equipment is clean and sanitized. Dissolve the mesophilic starter culture in 1/4 cup of cool, non-chlorinated water. If using pasteurized milk, dissolve the liquid calcium chloride in the same amount of water. Prepare the liquid rennet and annatto coloring, if using, and set them aside.
2. Heat the Milk: Pour the 2 gallons of milk into a large, non-reactive pot. Warm the milk over medium heat to 86°F (30°C), stirring occasionally to prevent scorching.
3. Add Starter Culture: Once the milk reaches 86°F, remove it from the heat. Stir in the dissolved mesophilic starter culture (and calcium chloride, if using) with an up-and-down motion for about 30 seconds.
4. Add Annatto Coloring: Stir in the liquid annatto coloring to achieve the desired red-orange color for Red Windsor cheese. Stir well to distribute the coloring evenly.
5. Add the Rennet: Gently stir in the diluted rennet solution for about 30 seconds to distribute it evenly throughout the milk.
6. Let the Curds Form: Cover the pot and let it sit undisturbed at room temperature for about 45-60 minutes, or until you achieve a clean break. The curds should have set and separated from the whey.
7. Cut the Curds: Use a long knife to cut the curds into small, uniform pieces, about the size of peas.
8. Stir and Cook the Curds: Place the pot back on the stove and gently heat the curds over low heat, stirring gently to prevent sticking. Slowly raise the temperature to 102°F (39°C) over the course of 30 minutes, stirring frequently.

9. Drain the Whey: Line a large colander with cheesecloth and place it over a clean sink or a large bowl. Carefully ladle the curds into the colander to drain off the whey.
10. Salt the Curds: Transfer the drained curds into a large mixing bowl and sprinkle them with cheese salt or kosher salt. Gently toss the curds to distribute the salt evenly.
11. Mold the Cheese: Line cheese molds with cheesecloth and transfer the salted curds into them. Press the curds gently into the molds, smoothing the surface.
12. Press the Cheese: Place a follower or plate on top of the cheese in each mold and press them at a light pressure for 12 hours.
13. Age the Cheese: After pressing, transfer the cheese to a cheese cave or refrigerator with a temperature of around 50-55°F (10-13°C) and moderate humidity. Age the cheese for at least 2-4 weeks, flipping it every few days and monitoring its progress.
14. Enjoy: Your homemade Red Windsor-style cheese is now ready to be enjoyed! Serve it on a cheese platter with fruit and crackers, melt it into dishes, or enjoy it on its own. Revel in the creamy texture and tangy flavor of your homemade cheese!

Sage Derby Cheese

Ingredients:

- 2 gallons whole cow's milk (preferably raw, but pasteurized milk can be used)
- 1/4 teaspoon mesophilic starter culture
- 1/4 teaspoon liquid calcium chloride (if using pasteurized milk)
- 1/4 teaspoon liquid rennet diluted in 1/4 cup cool, chlorine-free water
- 1/4 cup cool, chlorine-free water
- Cheese salt or kosher salt
- Fresh sage leaves or dried sage

Instructions:

1. Prepare Ingredients: Ensure all equipment is clean and sanitized. If using fresh sage leaves, finely chop them. Dissolve the mesophilic starter culture in 1/4 cup of cool, non-chlorinated water. If using pasteurized milk, dissolve the liquid calcium chloride in the same amount of water. Prepare the liquid rennet and set it aside.
2. Heat the Milk: Pour the 2 gallons of milk into a large, non-reactive pot. Warm the milk over medium heat to 86°F (30°C), stirring occasionally to prevent scorching.
3. Add Starter Culture: Once the milk reaches 86°F, remove it from the heat. Stir in the dissolved mesophilic starter culture (and calcium chloride, if using) with an up-and-down motion for about 30 seconds.
4. Add Sage: Add the chopped fresh sage leaves or dried sage to the milk and stir well to distribute evenly.
5. Add the Rennet: Gently stir in the diluted rennet solution for about 30 seconds to distribute it evenly throughout the milk.
6. Let the Curds Form: Cover the pot and let it sit undisturbed at room temperature for about 45-60 minutes, or until you achieve a clean break. The curds should have set and separated from the whey.
7. Cut the Curds: Use a long knife to cut the curds into small, uniform pieces, about the size of peas.
8. Stir and Cook the Curds: Place the pot back on the stove and gently heat the curds over low heat, stirring gently to prevent sticking. Slowly raise the temperature to 102°F (39°C) over the course of 30 minutes, stirring frequently.
9. Drain the Whey: Line a large colander with cheesecloth and place it over a clean sink or a large bowl. Carefully ladle the curds into the colander to drain off the whey.
10. Salt the Curds: Transfer the drained curds into a large mixing bowl and sprinkle them with cheese salt or kosher salt. Gently toss the curds to distribute the salt evenly.
11. Mold the Cheese: Line cheese molds with cheesecloth and transfer the salted curds into them. Press the curds gently into the molds, smoothing the surface.

12. Press the Cheese: Place a follower or plate on top of the cheese in each mold and press them at a light pressure for 12 hours.
13. Age the Cheese: After pressing, transfer the cheese to a cheese cave or refrigerator with a temperature of around 50-55°F (10-13°C) and moderate humidity. Age the cheese for at least 4-6 weeks, flipping it every few days and monitoring its progress.
14. Enjoy: Your homemade Sage Derby-style cheese is now ready to be enjoyed! Serve it on a cheese platter with fruit and crackers, or use it in sandwiches and salads. Revel in the creamy texture and subtle sage flavor of your homemade cheese!

Caerphilly Cheese

Ingredients:

- 2 gallons whole cow's milk (preferably raw, but pasteurized milk can be used)
- 1/4 teaspoon mesophilic starter culture
- 1/4 teaspoon liquid calcium chloride (if using pasteurized milk)
- 1/4 teaspoon liquid rennet diluted in 1/4 cup cool, chlorine-free water
- 1/4 cup cool, chlorine-free water
- Cheese salt or kosher salt

Instructions:

1. Prepare Ingredients: Ensure all equipment is clean and sanitized. Dissolve the mesophilic starter culture in 1/4 cup of cool, non-chlorinated water. If using pasteurized milk, dissolve the liquid calcium chloride in the same amount of water. Prepare the liquid rennet and set it aside.
2. Heat the Milk: Pour the 2 gallons of milk into a large, non-reactive pot. Warm the milk over medium heat to 86°F (30°C), stirring occasionally to prevent scorching.
3. Add Starter Culture: Once the milk reaches 86°F, remove it from the heat. Stir in the dissolved mesophilic starter culture (and calcium chloride, if using) with an up-and-down motion for about 30 seconds.
4. Add the Rennet: Gently stir in the diluted rennet solution for about 30 seconds to distribute it evenly throughout the milk.
5. Let the Curds Form: Cover the pot and let it sit undisturbed at room temperature for about 45-60 minutes, or until you achieve a clean break. The curds should have set and separated from the whey.
6. Cut the Curds: Use a long knife to cut the curds into small, uniform pieces, about the size of peas.
7. Stir and Cook the Curds: Place the pot back on the stove and gently heat the curds over low heat, stirring gently to prevent sticking. Slowly raise the temperature to 98°F (37°C) over the course of 30 minutes, stirring frequently.
8. Drain the Whey: Line a large colander with cheesecloth and place it over a clean sink or a large bowl. Carefully ladle the curds into the colander to drain off the whey.
9. Cheddar Curds Stage: After draining, return the curds to the pot and heat them to 100°F (38°C) while stirring. Once at temperature, turn off the heat and continue to stir for another 20 minutes.
10. Salting: Transfer the curds to a large bowl and sprinkle with cheese salt or kosher salt, mixing gently to ensure even distribution.
11. Molding: Line cheese molds with cheesecloth and transfer the salted curds into them. Press the curds gently into the molds, smoothing the surface.

12. Pressing: Place a follower or plate on top of the cheese in each mold and press them at a light pressure for 12 hours.
13. Aging: After pressing, remove the cheese from the molds, and air dry at room temperature for a day or two, turning occasionally. Then, wax the cheese and age it in a cool, humid environment (50-55°F or 10-13°C) for 3-6 weeks, turning it occasionally.
14. Enjoy: Your homemade Caerphilly cheese is now ready to be enjoyed! Serve it on a cheese platter, crumble it over salads, or enjoy it on its own. Revel in the crumbly texture and tangy flavor of your homemade cheese!

Dunlop Cheese

Ingredients:

- 2 gallons whole cow's milk (preferably raw, but pasteurized milk can be used)
- 1/4 teaspoon mesophilic starter culture
- 1/4 teaspoon liquid calcium chloride (if using pasteurized milk)
- 1/4 teaspoon liquid rennet diluted in 1/4 cup cool, chlorine-free water
- 1/4 cup cool, chlorine-free water
- Cheese salt or kosher salt

Instructions:

1. Prepare Ingredients: Ensure all equipment is clean and sanitized. Dissolve the mesophilic starter culture in 1/4 cup of cool, non-chlorinated water. If using pasteurized milk, dissolve the liquid calcium chloride in the same amount of water. Prepare the liquid rennet and set it aside.
2. Heat the Milk: Pour the 2 gallons of milk into a large, non-reactive pot. Warm the milk over medium heat to 86°F (30°C), stirring occasionally to prevent scorching.
3. Add Starter Culture: Once the milk reaches 86°F, remove it from the heat. Stir in the dissolved mesophilic starter culture (and calcium chloride, if using) with an up-and-down motion for about 30 seconds.
4. Add the Rennet: Gently stir in the diluted rennet solution for about 30 seconds to distribute it evenly throughout the milk.
5. Let the Curds Form: Cover the pot and let it sit undisturbed at room temperature for about 45-60 minutes, or until you achieve a clean break. The curds should have set and separated from the whey.
6. Cut the Curds: Use a long knife to cut the curds into small, uniform pieces, about the size of peas.
7. Stir and Cook the Curds: Place the pot back on the stove and gently heat the curds over low heat, stirring gently to prevent sticking. Slowly raise the temperature to 102°F (39°C) over the course of 30 minutes, stirring frequently.
8. Drain the Whey: Line a large colander with cheesecloth and place it over a clean sink or a large bowl. Carefully ladle the curds into the colander to drain off the whey.
9. Cheddar Curds Stage: After draining, return the curds to the pot and heat them to 100°F (38°C) while stirring. Once at temperature, turn off the heat and continue to stir for another 20 minutes.

10. Salting: Transfer the curds to a large bowl and sprinkle with cheese salt or kosher salt, mixing gently to ensure even distribution.
11. Molding: Line cheese molds with cheesecloth and transfer the salted curds into them. Press the curds gently into the molds, smoothing the surface.
12. Pressing: Place a follower or plate on top of the cheese in each mold and press them at a light pressure for 12 hours.
13. Aging: After pressing, remove the cheese from the molds, and air dry at room temperature for a day or two, turning occasionally. Then, wax the cheese and age it in a cool, humid environment (50-55°F or 10-13°C) for 2-4 months, turning it occasionally.
14. Enjoy: Your homemade Dunlop-style cheese is now ready to be enjoyed! Serve it on a cheese platter, slice it for sandwiches, or use it in your favorite recipes. Revel in the mild, buttery flavor and smooth texture of your homemade cheese!

Coolea Cheese

Ingredients:

- 2 gallons whole cow's milk (preferably raw, but pasteurized milk can be used)
- 1/4 teaspoon mesophilic starter culture
- 1/4 teaspoon liquid calcium chloride (if using pasteurized milk)
- 1/4 teaspoon liquid rennet diluted in 1/4 cup cool, chlorine-free water
- 1/4 cup cool, chlorine-free water
- Cheese salt or kosher salt

Instructions:

1. Prepare Ingredients: Ensure all equipment is clean and sanitized. Dissolve the mesophilic starter culture in 1/4 cup of cool, non-chlorinated water. If using pasteurized milk, dissolve the liquid calcium chloride in the same amount of water. Prepare the liquid rennet and set it aside.
2. Heat the Milk: Pour the 2 gallons of milk into a large, non-reactive pot. Warm the milk over medium heat to 86°F (30°C), stirring occasionally to prevent scorching.
3. Add Starter Culture: Once the milk reaches 86°F, remove it from the heat. Stir in the dissolved mesophilic starter culture (and calcium chloride, if using) with an up-and-down motion for about 30 seconds.
4. Add the Rennet: Gently stir in the diluted rennet solution for about 30 seconds to distribute it evenly throughout the milk.
5. Let the Curds Form: Cover the pot and let it sit undisturbed at room temperature for about 45-60 minutes, or until you achieve a clean break. The curds should have set and separated from the whey.
6. Cut the Curds: Use a long knife to cut the curds into small, uniform pieces, about the size of peas.
7. Stir and Cook the Curds: Place the pot back on the stove and gently heat the curds over low heat, stirring gently to prevent sticking. Slowly raise the temperature to 102°F (39°C) over the course of 30 minutes, stirring frequently.
8. Drain the Whey: Line a large colander with cheesecloth and place it over a clean sink or a large bowl. Carefully ladle the curds into the colander to drain off the whey.
9. Cheddar Curds Stage: After draining, return the curds to the pot and heat them to 100°F (38°C) while stirring. Once at temperature, turn off the heat and continue to stir for another 20 minutes.

10. Salting: Transfer the curds to a large bowl and sprinkle with cheese salt or kosher salt, mixing gently to ensure even distribution.
11. Molding: Line cheese molds with cheesecloth and transfer the salted curds into them. Press the curds gently into the molds, smoothing the surface.
12. Pressing: Place a follower or plate on top of the cheese in each mold and press them at a light pressure for 12 hours.
13. Aging: After pressing, remove the cheese from the molds, and air dry at room temperature for a day or two, turning occasionally. Then, wax the cheese and age it in a cool, humid environment (around 50-55°F or 10-13°C) for 2-6 months, turning it occasionally.
14. Enjoy: Your homemade Coolea-style cheese is now ready to be enjoyed! Serve it on a cheese platter, pair it with fruits and nuts, or use it in your favorite recipes. Revel in the rich, nutty flavor and smooth texture of your homemade cheese!

www.ingramcontent.com/pod-product-compliance
Lightning Source LLC
LaVergne TN
LVHW081605060526
838201LV00054B/2095